THE EYES OF FAITH

THE EYES OF FAITH

VEMPRE TERRELL, JR.

V. TERRELL
Grand Prairie, Texas

THE EYES OF FAITH
Published by:
V. Terrell
Grand Prairie, Texas
vempreterrell@utexas.edu

Vempre Terrell, Jr. / Editorial Director
Quality Press.info, Book Packager

ALL RIGHTS RESERVED

No parts of this book may be reproduced or transmitted in any form or by any means electronic or mechanical, including photocopying, recording or any information storage and retrieved system without the written permission from the author, except for the inclusion of brief quotations in review.

The publication is sold with the understanding that the Publisher is not engaged in rendering legal or other professional services. If legal advice or other expert assistance is required, the services of a competent professional person should be sought.

Copyright © 2017 by Vempre Terrell, Jr.
ISBN #978-1-937269-74-6
Library of Congress Control Number: 2017918273

DEDICATION

The Eyes of Faith is dedicated to you as the reader! God has a purpose behind every word that you will read during each second that you read this book. There will be no word in this book that you will stumble upon by accident. Our Heavenly Father wants you to know the strength of faith, and the power that it has when you allow it to move in your life.

ACKNOWLEDGEMENTS

I would like to take this time to first acknowledge my Heavenly Father for giving me the inspiration to write this book, so that it will serve as a motivational piece to other individuals. Also, I would like to thank my family for continuous encouragement in my life.

THE EYES OF FAITH

Through this eye-opening new book, Vempre Terrell, Jr. encourages readers to consider the physical and spiritual make up of a person's views: *the eyes*. This new book brings to light the reality that viewing life through faith serves as the blueprint of how blessings unfold. Having faith as the light behind your vision makes you see the best in all situations. By using THE EYES OF FAITH, you will find that what were once seen as hindrances become benefits that move you to unforeseen blessings. No matter what you happen to be going through, let THE EYES OF FAITH rest upon it with anticipation of triumphant blessings ahead!

TABLE OF CONTENTS

DEDICATION — i

ACKNOWLEDGEMENTS — iii

THE EYES OF FAITH — v

Chapter One — 1
    COME HELL OR HIGH WATER

Chapter Two — 37
    THE CALM IN THE STORM

Chapter Three — 68
    VICTORY RESIDES IN BELIEF

Chapter Four — 101
    THE HEARTBEAT OF TRIUMPH

ABOUT THE AUTHOR — 137

Chapter One

COME HELL OR HIGH WATER

How often does the word *never* come to mind for you? *Never* appears to be just another word in a sentence, but it carries much more meaning than what is understood on the surface. *I will **never** get this job. I will **never** be able to pay my car note. I will **never** live through this disease. I will **never** get into this school. I will **never** graduate from this school. I will **never** make it in this career. I will **never** make it through this day.* Now, just pay attention to how removing this one word changes the entire meaning of each sentence: *I will get this job. I will be able to pay my car note. I will live through this disease. I will get into this school. I will graduate from this school. I will make it in this career. I will make it through this day.* Each sentence was exactly the same as its previous mate, but with a slight, yet significant change. All it took was the removal of one word to change the entire meaning of each sentence. When the sentences did not have the word *never* as a part of their foundation, each of the other words came together to produce an entirely different outcome and interpretation.

I can say from personal experience that the word *never* has shown me its power in my own life. There have been times when I've entered situations thinking that things would *never* turn out in my favor. When this was the foundation of my thinking, the outcome sure enough turned out against me. As I sit here and recall times when I've applied to programs while thinking to myself, "I will *never* get into a program like this," I would then get rejection letters stating to me, "We regret to inform you…" After a while, it became second nature for me to believe that I was lacking something, and the word *never* became a strong part of how I viewed myself. Before I opened letters from programs where I greatly desired to be admitted, my mind would become bombarded with the thought, "I'll *never* get into this place," as my hands trembled with anticipation of rejection.

Looking down on myself finally became too much for me! I personally took a stand against being pessimistic toward myself, and I removed the word *never* from my mindset. I simply let the word *will* stand as the foundation of my goals. In doing so, I declared my success into existence by allowing *will* to link the words before and after it. With this, I could see myself being successful. I spoke success over my goals, before I even began to pursue them. I *will* be admitted into this program. I *will* get this job. I *will* make it through this illness. The doctor *will* come back with a good report. Thoughts like these became the guiding force of my goals. By embracing positive views of myself and my life, I was able to see myself move forward.

Doubt limits you to the background of defeat, but faith expands you to the forefront of excellence. Faith keeps you in the forefront, while doubt makes you fade into the background. Worrying that something will *never* happen limits you to the background of what you can do, but faith expands you to the forefront of what you *will* do. Faith brings you to the forefront of excellence through the favor of God. There are times in life when I've seen people who don't have the things that I have taken for granted in life, but they don't allow this to keep them in the background of what they are capable of doing in life. They look beyond what could limit them, and they move to greater heights in life.

Simply jogging through my community one afternoon provided me with the power of the life lesson of what happens when a person has removed the word *never* from his or her vocabulary. On this hot afternoon, I saw a man mowing the front yard of my neighbors' home. However, one thing quickly stood out to me about this man. He only had *one* arm. I was taken aback to see a man dripping in sweat, while mowing a yard with one arm, to ensure that he would have enough money to provide for himself and his family.

This experience touched me so much that I stopped jogging my normal route. I quickly went back home, and then jogged back to where the man was with a donation to give him. Once I returned, I stopped him from mowing to let him know that I had a donation to give him, and I was sure it would cover the amount of what he was doing. Adding to this, I let him know that I would mow the yard for him. He replied to me, "I cannot take this. I did not work for it. Thank you, Sir. Have a nice day." Next, the man continued mowing the yard as if there was no problem. Watching this man showed me the strength that comes to us when we don't allow a negative mindset to hold us back.

The way we view a situation carries a significant impact on its outcome before we even step into it. Viewing your circumstance as something that you will never conquer makes the circumstance conquer *you*, regardless of how capable you happen to be of conquering it. Just think of two people standing on the beach while viewing the waters of the ocean. Although both individuals happen to be looking at the *exact* same thing, what they see may be *totally* different.

One individual may see high waters that he will get on top of and use to surf from one point to another. On the other hand, the other individual may see the waters as something that he will never get on top of and never use to move from one point to another. Why? It's all because of one word: ***never***. The first individual sees high waters as something that he can use to move himself to greater heights in life. This is the type of person who does not see a challenge as something to back down from, but as something to stand up to in order to advance to higher places. That is the type of mindset that we must adopt in order to be successful. The next time you are faced with a challenge, let these words echo in your mind: *Come hell or high water, I'm advancing under God's power*! My friend, despite any setback that may attempt to hold you down, keep the faith that it is actually a setup for God to move you to greater heights.

Too often, we allow negative words to make us embrace negative viewpoints of a situation, and we let the discouragement that builds from it make us give up too soon on our goals. We tend to forget that life does not happen on our timetable. Life happens on God's timetable. Think about the last time you were waiting on an elevator that was just taking too long, from your point of view. Now, imagine walking outside, shortly after the elevator finally came for you, only to see a car accident in the very spot where you would have been if the elevator had come on your timetable. When all was said and done, you were not in that car accident because things happened on God's timetable, not yours.

The high waters of different challenges often present themselves in the same manner to different people. It is simply the way we view them that makes some individuals overcome challenges, while prompting others to succumb to them. How could one person be presented with a challenge and fall down to it, while another person is presented with the same challenge and triumph over it? One word stands behind the reasoning: *faith*. "Now faith is the substance of things hoped for, the evidence of things not seen" (Hebrews 11:1 KJV). Despite how difficult a challenge may appear, keep the faith! Having faith in the power of God to bless you paves the way for blessings to rain down upon you and balance the difficult waters of your life. There is never a misfortune too severe for you to surpass, when faith is what you use to view your life's circumstances.

Regardless of how challenging a set of circumstances may appear, do not just settle for less than what you know you can do. Answer uncertainty with faith. Answer doubt with hope. Answer insecurity with confidence. Come hell or high water, do not ever simply lie down to a challenge. There are so many times when success is so close within reach, yet we do not even realize it. Don't think of your circumstances from the viewpoint, "I'll *never*____." Think of your circumstances from the viewpoint, "I don't *yet* have____, but I *will* have____." Whatever it is that you are striving toward, keep the faith! Keep a positive viewpoint toward what you pursue in life. No matter how difficult a situation may appear at an everyday glance, do not give into accepting the defeated perspective of it.

My friend, the way we view things strongly affects the outcome of what is taking place. You may be looking at the same thing as someone else, but viewing it differently tends to produce an entirely different outcome. Just think of being asked, "How much gas is in your car?" You might reply, "Oh, it's half full" or "Oh, it's half empty," despite it being the same tank of gas that you're talking about. Although you are looking at the exact same thing, the *way* you look at it affects the outcome of your interpretation.

The eyes that you use to view your situations in life should not simply be your natural eyes. You should view your life's circumstances through the eyes of faith. Your faith should prompt a positive perspective upon whatever comes before you. When you see your life's situations simply through natural sight, the manner in which it would generally turn out is what you tend to see. On the other hand, when you see your life's situations through faith, you are able to see that the power of God will bless you to overcome any challenge that may come before you. With faith as your empowering view, you are able to walk with a strong step of confidence in the Lord. "For we walk by faith, not by sight" (2 Corinthians 5:7 KJV). Do not ever let the sight of the world be what guides you in life. Let the eyes of your faith in the power of the Lord be what leads and guides you every day of your life.

Many times, your confidence in your potential achievements may lessen as the high waters of life's challenges flood upon you. This may cause you to forget how capable you are of reigning upon the success that God has planned for you to achieve. "Cast not away therefore your confidence, which hath great recompense of reward" (Hebrews 10:35 KJV). Do not let hard times cause you to forget that you serve the all-powerful, true and living God. He has rewards waiting for you behind doors that you may have never dreamt would open. By viewing what is taking place in your life through the eyes of faith, you are able to guide yourself toward doors that God has planned to open for you.

Difficult times may cause one door to close in your life. However, do not forget that when faith in the Lord resides within you, multiple doors with better things behind them will open when one door closes. The new doors that open will have rewards for you behind them that will balance the flooding waters of the challenges that were formerly battling against you. My friend, you cannot forget that the way you view a situation is the driving force of the outcome. When faith is the light of your eye, a positive view floods upon your circumstances. The flooding of that positive view balances the high waters of any challenge.

Faith makes you see that no matter how difficult your life appears on the surface, God has a purpose for what you are going through. He has a plan to improve things for you. Once you step back to view your situation through the eyes of faith, you will see that you have come too far to give up on whatever goal you are pursuing, despite how difficult it appears to be to achieve it. My friend, the next time your burdens seem too much to bear, just think to yourself: *I have what it takes! I am good enough! God will bless me*! The pain that you endure from the challenges you withstand will prompt spiritual gain for success in your life.

Always keep in mind that your focus steers the vast majority of *what* will take place in your life, as well as *how* it will take place. A lack of focus tends to make you take an entirely different path than the one you wanted. Where does your focus rest? Does it begin with the negative? Does it stay on the negative? Does your focus begin with the positive? Does it rest upon the positive? What we focus upon may make us allow pessimism to overtake where optimism should rest. Just imagine being a student who receives grades, or being the parent of that student. You may see an A in one class, but a C in another class. Which grabs your attention more, the A or the C? From one viewpoint, you may see that what was done to make the A could be transferred to allow the C to become an A during the next grading period. From another viewpoint, your focus may reside upon the fact that something wrong was done to make the C. With this, you may never place any focus upon the A. This could cause you to overlook the positive points that brought about the A, and your unwavering focus on the C may even cause the A to lessen during the next grading period.

Even from my own personal standpoint, I have had a similar situation regarding grades happen in my life. Despite how positive the situation was, I still saw the negative in it, which I should not have done. I will never forget receiving my report card in high school with each of my grades as a 100 in every course, except a 97 in one of them. Although seven of my courses had a perfect score as the grade, one did not. For many people, this set of straight A's would have been perfect for them. For me, I was wondering what I did not do, due to me being three points away from perfection in *one* class. I wanted to know what I was lacking when it came to my understanding of the concepts. The way I was viewing the situation was from a negative perspective, not a positive one. Many other students could not understand what the problem was. For them, merely having a C in a course instead of having an F was something that they were celebrating. They were seeing the positive in their situations, while I was simply seeing the negative in mine.

Too often, we allow what demonstrates itself as the negative in our lives to supersede the positive. We do not see that the positive has the capability of transferring itself to make the negative also become positive. My friend, when a situation comes before you that appears to be negative, always strive to still see the positive in what is taking place. Step back and see what God is working to show you, in order for you to become a more prosperous person. Do your best to see what God is doing to move you to greater heights.

There are so many times when we let the negative points that we see at one moment override anything positive that may soon occur, or perhaps is already occurring. You cannot just give up because of how difficult a situation may seem at one point. Keep in mind that the future belongs to those who hold on to faith for victory to come to them in the future. Just think of the future few minutes. Quite a bit can happen in a few minutes.

Don't ever simply see the negative regarding what is happening in your life. God always has a purpose for what He is doing in your life. His plan may not appear reasonable to you, but always keep in mind that He is an on-time God. Our timing may not be His timing, but God's time is always the right time!

Something may appear to be taking too long to happen on your time scale, and you may just want to throw in the towel and give up right now. Even so, before you give up, always ask yourself, "If I stop right now, will I be satisfied with the outcome?" The timing may be stretched because God is using extra time to make you see something new. Our Heavenly Father may have something different to show you from what you have already seen. Just think of the last time you watched a movie that you had already seen. Even though you had seen it before, just picture one different thing that you saw the second time, but you did not see the first time. How is it that you could see something *different* than you saw the first time? Why wasn't *everything* you saw *exactly* the same? It is because nothing is ever the same *every* time. Anytime you look at the same thing a second time, there is always something different to find that you did not see the first time. That is often why God presents something to you a second time. God puts it in front of you again for a reason. God does nothing on accident. He does everything on purpose, for a purpose, and with a purpose. The Lord always has a purpose for His plan.

Keep the faith! Holding on just another day, another hour, another minute, or even another second may be all that it takes to see your blessings flow upon you. Learning from yesterday helps you move forward. Standing for today gives you hope. Looking toward tomorrow makes you keep the faith. Do not let discouragement overtake your spirit. Allow encouragement to be what dwells within you. When you look at each situation that comes before you through the eyes of faith, you embrace an attitude of expectancy. With an attitude of expectancy living within your spirit, you are able to look toward God's excellence unfolding in your life, regardless of how your situations may appear.

The manner in which you view your circumstances dictates your understanding of the outcome. "Trust in the LORD with all thine heart; and lean not unto thine own understanding. In all thy ways acknowledge Him, and He shall direct thy paths" (Proverbs 3:5-6 KJV). When your personal understanding is what controls your mindset, what you see will be steered by the natural. On the other hand, when your trust in the Lord is what steers your spirit, your faith will overcome your simple understanding of the natural mindset.

You must remember that the eyes are the window to triumph or defeat. When faith is what you use to view life's happenings, triumph is what stands before you. At the same time, when worldly eyes are what you use to view life's happenings, defeat is what awaits you. What is taking place today may not seem fair. It may appear as if nothing will ever take place in your favor. However, remember that God is always in control of every situation. Having faith in Him, is what makes the tide turn in your favor.

I will never overcome this problem. I do not have what it takes. I cannot win this game. I might as well quit now. I probably will not get this job. Are these the types of comments about yourself that come to mind as life pans out for you? If so, you are already defeated before you even begin to pursue what you are moving toward. You may be the best, most talented individual in your field, but you will not realize it if you do not first believe it yourself.

You must first believe what you can do before you will realize success from any great point. From my own personal experience, I have even seen this to be true. There were so many local and regional public speaking competitions in which I won first place. However, when I came to the national level, I felt this was too high of an area for me to be the best. I did not think I was the best in the nation when it came to public speaking. With this, although I recited the exact same speech that I wrote and won many awards for previously, I did not even place at the national level. Countless people asked me questions along these lines: *What happened? Why weren't you as good as you normally are?* When I stepped back to see the situation from the eyes of my admiring audience members, I could not understand why I did not see *myself* as well as I normally did when performing my speeches.

A few years later, I took the time to enter another national contest. The difference this time was that I had a great level of belief in myself to become a national award winner. Soon after, I received a letter stating that I was chosen as a national award winner. As I read the words of the letter recognizing me as a national award winner, I was in utter amazement. I could hear the words of our Heavenly Father speaking to me: "You must first believe in yourself before anyone else will believe in you!"

The store associated with this national award put posters of me in multiple locations throughout the country. As I stood in one store location, a small child looked at me, then he looked at the poster. While pointing back and forth at the poster and at me, the child then turned to his mother and enthusiastically declared, "Mommy, that's that man!" His mother was appalled and embarrassed that her son was having such a fit over me. She quickly turned to her son and said, "Don't point at people, you know that's not...that *is* that man! Sir, we're so sorry. We are just so shocked to see you in person!"

An experience like this would never have come about if I had not first believed in myself to gain triumph at the top. Although it was a challenge for me to be chosen by the committee over so many others throughout the country, God had this blessing planned for me. All I had to do, on my part, was have faith that I would receive the blessing. I had to believe in myself before anyone else would believe in me.

No challenge will be overcome when you believe that you do not have what it takes to triumph over it. Challenges come from high waters in order to serve as a setup for better times ahead. As long as faith dwells within you, the excellence of any situation will be what you see ahead, despite what may be taking place in your life at this very second.

Overcoming adversity is something that I have had to do from birth. With oxygen deprivation being a major medical setback in my delivery at birth, doctors began to believe the worst for me. From the medical view that the doctors held, I would either die within a matter of hours, or be severely mentally challenged throughout my life. Even with the high waters of this adversity flowing over me, my family chose to see the situation through the eyes of faith instead of failure. Not only have I lived greatly beyond the small frame of time that I was given, I have also been blessed to be highly accomplished from an intellectual standpoint. At this time, I am a graduate of one of the most well-known universities in the nation, the University of Texas at Austin.

Too often in life, the high waters of adversity will do their best to make you fall. However, you cannot allow that to happen in order to triumph over the tides of trouble. There is nothing in life that is *meant* for you that will not take place, no matter what challenges may present themselves before you. To know that I am sitting here at this very moment writing the words of this book reaffirms my belief to see life through the eyes of faith, not through worldly eyes. This shows me that despite the doctors at my time of birth pessimistically communicating the message to my family that I would never be able to do something of this nature, God still had plans for me beyond the limitations of the world.

Times of adversity may prompt doubt and uncertainty to manifest in the minds of even the most focused, goal-oriented people. Nevertheless, the seeds of doubt that begin to come about within the inner psyche of an individual are the result of viewing life through the eyes of the world, not through the eyes of a child of God. The eyes of a worldly individual may simply see the negative effects of a disease, the pessimistic consequences of a job loss, the detrimental results of a relationship ending, or any other unfavorable situation. Even so, the spiritual eyes of a child of God see far *beneath* the surface of what appear to be strictly negative results that life experiences bring.

In order to overcome the adversities that arise in life, you must learn to not just give up because of what your physical eyes happen to see at one particular period of time. You must step back from the natural and allow your spiritual side to permit you to look through the eyes of your faith. When you do this, you will see that God is in the driver's seat of whatever ride you are taking at this time, no matter how it may seem.

Do not let go of the reality that God is in control of your life. God knows who you are. God knows where you are. God knows what you are. God knows what you are capable of doing. There is nothing within you that God is not aware is there. He has placed everything within you that is within you. Too often, we forget this. My friend, you cannot close your eyes to seeing success ahead of you, as a result of the power of our Heavenly Father.

When you open the eyes of your faith to excellence as the outcome of whatever is taking place now in your life, you let go of *thinking* that God *may* bring your blessings to pass. You then *know* that God *will* bring your blessings to pass! Once you allow your faith to outshine the natural, you are able to see God's work. Our Father not only makes the impossible become possible, He also makes the impossible become reality.

Discouragement may dwell within your spirit at this time. Thoughts of doubt may manifest themselves in your mind. Despite this, hold strong to your faith. By doing this, your attitude of expectancy in the power of God to bless you will steer you away from failure and toward success. Walk upright with an attitude of faith that your blessings are coming. Regardless of what may be taking place now, keep a stance of thankfulness. Let thanksgiving already be present within you for the blessings that you know you will receive before you receive them.

Please understand that every situation will not be a great situation. The Lord does take the time to test you to see if you truly believe that you will receive your blessings. He wants to display for you if your belief outweighs your uncertainty.

No matter how unfair a situation in your life may appear, you must keep the faith that God will bless you to overcome it. We all experience unfair situations in life. As I sit here writing this book, many unfair situations that have taken place in my life rush to mind for me. However, many blessings that have served as the outcomes of my unfair situations function as examples for me of what faith does in times of adversity. While in the midst of life's bad breaks, do not dwell upon the shortcomings of the situations. Please do not make the mistake of only seeing the negative aspects of a situation.

Despite how times in your life seem for you at this moment, always keep in mind that faith is what moves you toward your season of triumph. No one will always endure hard times. Hard times serve as a lesson that God is using to empower you to achieve greatness. There is a purpose behind every season that our Heavenly Father allows to happen in your life. Added to this, there is a time for every occurrence in your life. "To everything there is a season, and a time to every purpose under the heaven" (Ecclesiastes 3:1 KJV). The season of your blessings is ahead. Never give up on the greatness that awaits you. Stay in faith. Let hope live within you. Hold strong to the belief that God will move mountains on your behalf, despite what those mountains happen to be.

It is often too easy to let the eyes of man steer you toward the fear of failure so much that you embrace failure and lead yourself to it. You cannot succumb to this negative mindset. Remember that the eyes of God are looking down upon you, even in the midst of the eyes of man looking at you. Viewing life's situations through the eyes of faith shows this to especially be true. Faith is the agent of change that man cannot deter when it serves as your connection to the Lord. Knowing this, although the eyes of man may be upon you at one point in time, just remember that the eyes of God are upon you for all of eternity! When you realize that God's eyes are watching you at all times, both good and bad, you are able to view life through the eyes of faith.

My friend, do not allow facing a challenge to lessen your purpose in life. God has a meaning for every moment that takes place in your life. He challenges you for the better, so that you will become better. Our Heavenly Father encourages you to be better. It may appear that your dream for one achievement in life has died. Nevertheless, God may have put that dream to rest, in order for you to take hold of an even better dream.

While one dream may no longer live, keep the assurance within you that God still has greatness planned to pan out in your life. At one point in time, you may have had the dream of becoming a world-renowned neurosurgeon. Regardless of this, that dream may have died. Despite that dream no longer living, God may then place the dream within your heart to become a highly accomplished attorney. Being an attorney may then allow you to bring freedom to a client who may have been wrongly convicted if you had not become an attorney, instead of following your original desire of being a neurosurgeon. Even when one dream dies, God always has another great one waiting for you. Any challenge you may face always has blessings behind it. All it takes on your part is to keep the faith for blessings to be the outcome of the challenge.

No challenge is ever set forth without a reason. There is always a purpose behind every challenge that comes about in your life. Challenges are placed before you with God's reasoning of teaching a lesson. You may not realize that you have a gift that is hidden within you. However, a challenge that comes before you may be what God uses to allow that gift to manifest itself.

We don't always realize why challenges present themselves in our lives, but the Lord brings forth His reasoning in the form of greatness. Keep in mind that although we may not know why things are taking place at one particular point, the Lord always lets us know in Heavenly time. The Lord's time is *always* the *right* time. Regardless of what you may not understand now in the face of your challenges, the Lord always has your blessings prepared for you, when all is said and done.

It may appear to you that although you get down on your knees each night in prayer, nothing is coming forth as a result of it. You may think to yourself: *I'm wasting my time doing this. Prayer doesn't work. No one hears me when I do this.* My friend, don't think that nothing comes about when you speak to God. He is listening. His plans await you. You simply need to keep the faith. Believe that you will receive your blessings. Just think to yourself: *My blessings are waiting for me. Excellence will take place in my life. I just need to keep the faith.*

Don't think that the bad breaks of yesterday will hold you back today. Don't let yesterday block your footsteps forward today. A fall back yesterday is not nearly as important as a set up for the blessings ahead of you today. Never allow doubts of what you are capable of doing tomorrow to lessen the value of what you can do today. "Yesterday is a cancelled check; tomorrow is a promissory note; today is the only cash you have, so spend it wisely" — Kay Lyons. There is no reason why you should let today be a time when you permit uncertainty to overpower your capabilities. The here and now is right in front of you, and the only thing stopping you from pursuing whatever it is that you want to pursue is *you*.

Too often people spend most of their time waiting for tomorrow. They concentrate so much on tomorrow that they don't appreciate today. Many people don't use today to move toward success tomorrow. There are so many individuals who live in discouragement today, because they dislike the present. You cannot embrace that type of mindset. Despite the discouragement that may be urging you to push toward tomorrow and disregard today, faith is an entity of the present tense. There must first be faith within you today, in order for you to reach new heights tomorrow. To become greater tomorrow, you must first keep the faith today.

Allow yourself to expand at the very place where you are now, despite how undesirable your present circumstances may appear. Expanding yourself today is the key to reaching greater heights tomorrow. If you were already at the greater heights where God planned for you to be, there would be no need to keep the faith in order for you to move higher. You would simply remain at the status quo. There would be no need to have a desire for progress.

God has you where you are right now for a reason. You are where you are because you are moving on God's timeline. Times today may seem to be too much to bear, but never hang your head in defeat. Keep the faith! Let go of your fears, and let God balance the waves of limitations in your life.

Be the best that you can be today. Be the best that you can be at this very moment. Be the best *you* that you can be right now. When you do your best today, you will be even better tomorrow. Don't let your focus reside upon comparing yourself to others. Don't see what someone else has as something that you lack. Whatever you have today is what you are supposed to have today, no more, no less. Focus upon your high points. Focus upon the greatness within you. Focus upon being your best. Focus upon why your best is *your* best, and how it can make you even greater.

If God wasn't working to teach you a lesson, He would not have you where you are with what you have. Don't rush through today. Embrace today. Embrace the present, and let God mold your happenings in His time for the future. Just keep this spiritual declaration in mind: *I'm going to be the best that I can be today! Then, I will be an even better form of my best tomorrow!*

Let faith be what guides you toward being your best, despite how the natural eye may see your current circumstances. Don't let the sight of the natural eye keep you from blossoming today, and blossoming even more tomorrow. Blossom even further into your best, despite how your situation may seem at this second. Flourish in your current soil.

Take your time. Live one day at a time. Enjoy today. Today is not here for nothing. There is a purpose for today. There is a reason why God placed today on the calendar of your life. Take the steps of today with confidence! Let your steps today lead you into many new blessings tomorrow. "The steps of a good man are ordered by the Lord: and he delighteth in his way" (Psalm 37:23 KJV). God has you where you are for a reason. He has you taking the steps that you will take for a reason. Our Heavenly Father simply wants you to take steps of faith so that you will step up to your blessings. He wants you to step out on faith, despite what may be standing in front of you.

Make your best effort to step into positive places. Strive to position yourself into a positive atmosphere. Let the steps of your faith guide you to an environment where advancements will come to you. The place where your faith allows you to step into has a big impact on the places where you will be in the future. Make your best effort to step into a setting where you will be able to blossom. Let your faith shine through you with each step you take, despite how difficult the challenges before you happen to be.

When faith dwells within you, there is substance behind what you hope to achieve, and evidence of your blessings ahead, regardless of what you may not have already achieved. Just think of the many athletic programs that gain so much attention on an everlasting basis. If you were an athlete, why would you go to practice each day? Why would you put in extra effort outside of practice to stand out to the countless fans of the sport? You might put forth all of your possible effort, in and out of practice, and lose the game. With that in mind, why would you even put forth the effort to win? It is all because of one word: *faith*. When faith lives inside of you, you are able to see the situation through the eyes of faith. You are able to set your feet on the field, with the belief that you will walk off as a winner. You are able to step on the court, with the belief in your heart that you will win. You are able to walk onto the course, knowing that your win will be what the fans will be talking about, when all is said and done.

Keep the faith! Let faith be the viewpoint from which you look, as you see what takes place in your life. Have hope within your heart to overcome whatever challenge may arise before you. Let encouragement overpower your discouragement, all the days of your life, even the bad days. High tides of trouble may make it seem like: *This is just a waste of time. I might as well give up now. I might as well throw my hands up and forget this. I'll never win this battle.* Don't embrace thoughts like these. Never let these beliefs overtake your spirit. Despite what "this" happens to be, do not let "this" make you believe that you do not have what it takes to come out on top when your faith resides in the power of God.

Shake off the disappointments of yesterday. Stand up for the greatness that may come into your life today. Embrace a positive attitude, no matter what may be taking place in your life. No one has ever experienced only high points in life, not even Jesus Christ himself. So many people have pursued goals only to be overwhelmed with disappointments. Just think of a college student who set foot on the grounds of a college campus with great thoughts of a future career, only to have disappointments seemingly tear down those initial goals. Imagine being one of the top students of your high school; you confidently go to a university in pursuit of a career. Then, your grades are released at the end of the first grading period, leading to utter disappointment. You might see the glass half empty at that point. You could believe that you don't have what it takes to become a college graduate. On the other hand, you could step back from the situation and see the glass half full, which would drive you where you need to be in order to become a graduate.

Don't look at any happening in life as a mere disappointment. See it as a lesson that God is working to teach you. There is always a purpose behind what God does. Keep in mind that whatever is taking place in your life, it is not what God is doing *to* you; it is what He is doing *for* you. As you view hard times through the eyes of faith, you will see high tides of trouble from a much different perspective. Think of a career you may have. Although you may struggle daily with a career that is highly related to mathematics, it may be because God is working to show you that He has an even better path waiting for you. It may be God's way of having you to step away from your mathematically-related career, and starting a business of your own. God may be striving to show you that you are highly gifted when it comes to running your own business. After letting go of the mathematically-related career that you had and starting your own business, you may go from being an employee making $38,000 a year to a CEO making $250,000 a year. That's quite a jump that never would have taken place if everything would have simply been fine for you in the way that you wanted.

Always take the time to listen to God. Always step back to see what God is working to show you. Always give true thought to what God is speaking through your situation. Always keep in mind that God uses setbacks as setups for even better points to come about in our lives. Always let faith remind you that a bad day today will not hold you back from better days ahead.

From many views, college is a key feature of success as an adult. Imagine being a young man who comes from the household of a struggling mother. With this, not only are you striving to move forward for yourself, but you are also striving to move forward to help your mother. While your friends simply see being outside playing sports as preparation to "go pro," you see it as preparing yourself to stand out enough to receive a college scholarship. Nevertheless, you don't merely want your scholarship to make you "just another athlete." It is your goal to use the scholarship to finance your education.

You may work so hard each day to become a better wide receiver, but it may appear that the harder you work, the worse you become. Even so, that may simply be God's way of showing you that it is not in His plan for you to be a part of the offense. It may be in His plan for you to be a part of the defense. Now, imagine that on your first game night as a cornerback on defense, a significant college recruiter sees you in action and has to have you. After that, you then receive the much-needed college scholarship. This sets you up to gain the education that you need to follow the career path that you are working toward. Following this, you are able to help yourself by means of having a six-figure salary as a corporate executive, as well as help bring your mother out of financial poverty.

While on the subject of college, imagine that you are a struggling high school student who sees college as what will bring greatness into your life. So many people may have told you things like: *You're not smart enough. You don't have what it takes. You'll never make it in college.* Next, picture yourself working hard each afternoon, during tutoring, to grasp the concepts of the subjects in which you struggle, followed by going home to study to further your understanding, even more. Now, imagine receiving grades consistently high enough to make you receive a greatly needed academic scholarship. To take it a step further, imagine walking across the stage on your college graduation day, as they call your name. At this point, visualize the same people, who told you that you would never make it in college, coming into your office in need of your services after you become a college graduate. My friend, it's not what other people believe about you. It's what *you* believe about yourself.

There are so many people who are easily able to tell you what you can't do, regardless of how well they do or don't know you. However, the same people who are bold enough to speak poorly of you don't have the nerve to take a stand for what they believe in themselves. These same "strong" individuals, who are quick to speak down upon others, are slow to stand up for their beliefs. Just picture a veteran, who a bully significantly spoke down upon in his younger years, returning from defending his country. Imagine that one of the first people who the veteran sees upon his return is the bully who previously did his best to tear the veteran down. Picture the veteran in his ensemble that he wore in defense of the country, as he simply looks at the bully in his everyday outfit.

The veteran would not have to say a word, because a look from the veteran to the bully would be worth a thousand words. Just being in his ensemble, which was worn in defense of the country, speaks to the bully that the veteran was willing to put his life on the line for the country. The knowledge that the veteran was willing to stand up for his country shows that he is not at all the weak person the bully attempted to point out to others. Believing in himself showed the veteran that he was not the weak person who the bully endeavored to illustrate to others. Faith empowered the veteran to look beyond the bully, boldly go overseas, fight for his country, and return as a hero for his country.

Let your belief in the fact that you have whatever it takes for you to succeed be an encouragement for you each day. Expect the favor of God to flood upon you at any moment. It may not be at the moment that you expect it, but it will be the right moment. God's favor always comes at the right moment. The favor of God makes blessings rain down upon us so much that the tides of trouble become still, and our blessings bring about excellence in our lives. Let hope live within you. Let faith be what guides you. Expect greatness to come about for you.

Pause for a moment with me. Close your eyes. Reflect upon one experience in your life when something difficult was taking place. Let this be a difficult time when you were unsure of the outcome. Let this be a time when you struggled to overcome a challenge, in which doubt did its best to make you believe that the challenge would overcome you, instead of you overcoming the challenge. However, let this be a time when you overcame the challenge. Allow the time in question when you overcame this challenge to set the standard for your belief that you have what it takes to be successful against *any* challenge that you may come up against.

My friend, as you can see just from reflecting upon that situation in your life, you do have what it takes to triumph over challenges. You are not merely wasting your time standing up against hard times. You have more than just *a* chance to come out on top. You have *the* chance. Never think that God has put something within your heart for no reason. Our Heavenly Father always has a purpose for what He does. Hold strong to the knowledge that the troublesome tides of challenges may happen to be blessings in disguise that are headed your way. Allow your disappointments to serve as encouragements for your next great step in life.

The high waters that challenges bring with them often tend to be what God uses to move us beyond a stagnant state of life. Being where you are at this point in time may seem to be so great that you do not want one change to take place. Even so, God may have better plans for you than you could ever imagine. Your current point may be far below where God has planned for you to be. For our Heavenly Father to breathe life into His plans for our lives, it often takes one word that is the best friend of some and the worst enemy of others: *change*. Change tends to be highly embraced by those who see other places for themselves that are different from where they currently are. On the same token, change is often something that others do their best to push aside. It may be because they are content with where they are, or because they are afraid to step beyond the current path that they are following. Never simply view change as a hardship. When God brings change into your life, He always has a purpose.

Disappointments of yesterday, challenges of today, and uncertainties of tomorrow are not intended to tear you down. Times like these are meant to build strength within your spirit, build strength within your faith, and make you strong enough to take a stand against any challenge that may present itself before you. Don't think that hard times are too much for you to handle. Don't think that hard times are happening without a reason. Don't think that hard times come about to make you give up on your blessings. You have every ounce of what it takes within you to move beyond whatever the hard times are that you are enduring. One word sums up what it takes for you to win the battle against your hard times: *faith*.

You and I have both had challenges to overcome. We've had hard times to endure. These hard times often tend to be what God uses to illustrate the greatness that He has within His power, and the greatness that He has placed within us to overcome these hard times. The high waters of hard times often serve as the test to a dream. They are testing how much we want a blessing. Sometimes God urges you to throw the Hail Mary of hope behind your dream in order to make it happen. As you do so, keep the substance of hope behind that Hail Mary as you maintain your belief that the dream will come to pass.

When difficult periods make what were once hopeful dreams in your life become tarnished dreams, don't simply let go of those dreams without a fight. Take the time to see if those dreams are what God wants you to have. Take the time to see what God is striving to show you in terms of the hard times that have come along with those dreams. Take the time to see from the eyes of your faith the picture that God is painting for you. As you take the time to see what God is working to show you, this allows you to see that the disappointment that lives beside your hard times is there because God's work is still in action. He is still building the bridge from a low area in your life to a much higher one. Don't let the frustration with the timing of your blessings make you give up on being blessed. Keep the faith! Don't give up! When you keep the faith, disappointments become appointments with greatness. When you keep the faith, a loss at one point becomes a much greater gain at another. When you keep the faith, God uses the setbacks in your hard times as set ups to greater heights.

Blessings do not end because of one loss. Life does not end because of one loss. Let the losses that occur in your life lead you to much greater wins. Right now, it may seem difficult to encourage yourself to see better times ahead. You may think to yourself, "If faith will bring so many blessings in my life, why don't I see any of them now?" Don't let negative thoughts like these overpower your thinking. Don't let doubts take hold of your spirit. Always keep in mind that your blessings are already lined up in accordance with God's timing. His plans are already written to make your tests become testimonies of your blessings. Our Heavenly Father is simply asking for one thing from you: *faith*. No matter what may be taking place in your life, let your belief in the power of God turn your frustrations into faith.

Let your faith serve as a declaration of success. Each morning that you take in the breath of a new day, affirm these words to yourself: *God has great things prepared for me today!* No matter how big or small these things may seem to the natural eye, always see through the eyes of your faith the excellence that God has prepared for you. Encourage yourself to expect blessings that God has prepared for you.

Instead of settling with failure, expect your blessings. Instead of setting with mediocrity, expect your blessings. Instead of settling with the status quo, expect your blessings. Instead of settling below where you know God wants you to be, expect your blessings. No matter what may be taking place at this moment, or what has already taken place, nothing is an accident. God does not make mistakes. Our Heavenly Father will change what appears to be a mistake into a miracle in your life. He has brought each second in your life about in the manner that it has unfolded for a reason.

When the high tides of trouble seem to be too much to bear, hold your head up. Look your troubles straight in the eye through the eyes of your faith, and don't settle for defeat. Put a smile on your face, and keep in mind that God will bless you to finish the race. Regardless how high the tides of a challenge may appear to be, keep the faith that God will bless you with victory.

Chapter Two

THE CALM IN THE STORM

The storms of life often come with such a rage that it is difficult to imagine that you will ever be able to overcome them. Hope to surpass hard times is often something that many people convince themselves that they do not have, and they cannot obtain. Despite this, never let life's circumstances cause you to look down upon yourself. Let the courage within your soul encourage you to have the spiritual audacity to hope for overpowering any challenge that may present itself before you. With substance behind the audacity of hope with your spirit, you will see yourself move to greater heights than you may have never imagined you would reach. Do not give up on the belief that the hard times of today cannot be surpassed. "There is surely a future hope for you, and your hope will not be cut off" (Proverbs 23:18 NIV). When hope is alive within you, your belief in being your best also lives within you. When hope manifests itself through you, your challenges are illustrated to you as lessons from God of His glory when it comes to what He allows you to rise above.

To have the courage to hope for better times ahead of your current challenges, you must properly view what is in front of you. Grasping a worldly view tends to be what causes the negative to overpower the positive in your life. It makes pessimism overpower optimism. Viewing a challenge through worldly eyes takes away gladheartedness in the midst of hard times. It makes you forget that despite troubles taking place, there are always positive lessons to be learned. Regardless how difficult your current set of circumstances may seem, step back and see what the Lord is striving to show you. Look at your circumstances through the eyes of faith, not the eyes of the world. Let faith be what steers your focus. Take joy in the lessons that the Lord is teaching you.

> **"Life is not about waiting for the storm to pass; it's about learning to dance in the rain."**
> **—Vivian Greene**

When you look at your problems through the eyes of faith, you enlarge the vision of greatness ahead of you. As a result, you see wins taking place on your behalf that are far above the natural means. These are wins from the supernatural power of God.

By viewing each situation through the eyes of faith, we are able to see a win in every situation, good or bad. It is so easy to thank God when we are winning in life, despite if we are looking through the natural eye or the faithful eye. If we have been given a promotion, we find it easy to thank Him for this. If we have received gains in our finances, we find it easy to thank Him for this. Why? It is because these are situations that everyone views as being prosperous. These are wins to the natural eye. On the same token, do you still thank God when things are not going well for you?

We cannot just be thankful to the Lord in the best of times. My friend, we must also be thankful to Him even in the worst of times, no matter how badly they seem on the surface. "In everything give thanks; for this is the will of God in Christ Jesus for you" (1 Thessalonians 5:18 NKJV). Some people find it difficult to thank the Lord in challenging times. Despite this, it is in these times that we learn that there is a true difference between having *joy* and having *happiness*. Life's hard times reveal to us that while *joy* and *happiness* are often terms that are used synonymously, they most certainly do not carry the same meaning.

Difficult times in life make the difference between *joy* and *happiness* clearly known. *Happiness* describes good feelings that take place within a person when life's happenings are going well. The emotion of happiness is contingent upon the positive happenings that are taking place in life. As long as things are going well for you, happiness stays strong within you. On the other hand, joy is a gift within the spirit that comes from Jesus. This gift continually inspires and motivates your faith. "Consider it pure joy, my brothers and sisters, whenever you face trials of many kinds, because you know that the testing of your faith produces perseverance" (James 1:2-3 NIV).

Joy is the feeling of inner harmony that Jesus bestows upon us, which allows us to smile even in the face of adversity. Joy reminds us that it takes more muscles to frown than it does to smile. Joy is an emotion that makes us have a glow in our eyes, even though times may be hard. Joy is an emotion of the spirit that Jesus gives to His people, and the world cannot take it away! When the Lord gives you a gift, nobody can take it away! Through the inner harmony that Jesus gives you, you'll have joy in your heart from the dawn of the morning to the midnight hour.

While happiness may be shattered by foul happenings that take place, joy stands strong in the midst of life's difficulties. Bad news that comes about may turn months of happiness into years of sadness, which shows that this is not an emotion that is a direct gift from Jesus. Though joy and happiness may momentarily be confused if you don't know the true meaning of each, life's lessons certainly make it known that there is a tremendous distinction between the two.

Having joy within you illustrates in your mind the importance of giving God praise and expressing thanks to Him. It stirs the need within your spirit to uplift His name.

"O magnify the LORD with me, and let us exalt His name together" (Psalm 34:3 KJV). I cannot say enough that giving praise to the Lord is how we connect with Him. Exalting our Heavenly Father brings forth the power within us to keep the faith to stand up against any challenge. "I will bless the LORD at all times: his praise shall continually be in my mouth" (Psalm 34:1 KJV). Give God praise in both good times and bad. Let the words that flow from your mouth serve as a manner in which you build your connection with the Lord. Let your words of praise strengthen the faith within you.

The more you have words of praise flow from your tongue, the stronger the power within you exists to put negative words and views of others to rest. "Death and life are in the power of the tongue: and they that love it shall eat the fruit thereof" (Proverbs 18:21 KJV). When you allow another person's negative words to become a part of your thoughts, you give them power over you. You give that person control over you. You make that person a part of you. Don't let another person lessen your perception of yourself. Don't let another person lessen your view of what you can do. Don't let another person lessen your faith. Tune out their negative words, and tune into your expectations for God's greatness to unfold in your life.

Others may see your challenge as something that you will never surpass. They may see you as someone who does not have what it takes to be victorious. Despite how other people may see you, still keep the faith. Believe that you will triumph over any challenge that presents itself before you. See the challenge as a step that will promote you to the blessings that God has planned for you to receive. View the challenge as something that God is not only using to place you on a path to greater heights, but also as something for you to put your negative critics to shame. Let your negative critics see that excellence is the outcome when you are a child of God.

Keep in mind that God has the power to cause those who said you would never make it to have to come to you in need — something that they never would have imagined to be possible, much less to become reality. Just keep the faith. Believe in your heart that success is ahead of you. Believe in your spirit that greatness is coming to you. Despite how difficult your circumstances may seem, hold strong to a mindset of faith and expectancy.

Regardless how negative the words of others may seem against you, still keep the faith that the time for your blessings is ahead. Simply because a blessing has not come about in your manner of time does not mean that you won't receive it. Remember that just as there are seasons designated for each set of months, there are also seasons designated for each point of our lives. God uses certain seasons to prepare us to receive our blessings. He uses others to allow us to grow with the receipt of our blessings. While the negative words of others may seem to simply tear you down, take the time to stop and see the positive effects that antagonistic words may have upon you.

When you see yourself in a positive manner, what others say does not have the power to tear you down. Let the words that you speak about yourself have greater power upon your life than the words of others. Let the way you view yourself have greater power over your life than the views of others. My friend, pause for a moment here with me. Take the time to look in the mirror. As you look at yourself, speak these words into existence: *I see a great work of God! I see a masterpiece! I see God's excellence at work!*

Don't ever permit any person's negative views of you to become views that you adopt of yourself. When man tries to rain on your parade, just remember that the Lord reigns above everything and everyone. Besides, the reign of the Lord beats the rain of man's negative prophecies in any weather forecast. Jesus is your sunlight in the midst of rain. He is your strength in the midst of the storm. Jesus is the reason for every season, and He can steer the weather during any time to shift in favor of you.

My friend, no matter how badly a situation may appear today, you must remember that Jesus is the fortress that protects you against any and all troubles in life that may arise against you. Don't fall prey to the tricks of Satan. The works of Satan are at work to make you believe that God will not have your blessings to shower down upon you. Turn away from Satan's tricks, and turn to the Word of God. Let righteousness live within your spirit, and walk upright by means of your beliefs in the power of God. "The path of the righteous is like the morning sun, shining even brighter till the full light of day" (Proverbs 4:18 NIV). As you righteously walk with the Lord, His favor will shine upon you.

As the storms of trouble crash upon you, it is so easy to let go and give up on your goals. *What is the purpose of looking forward when it seems that hard times are the main point in life at this moment?* In the midst of viewing life through the natural eye, you are prone to see life through the rearview mirror, and questions of this sort begin to overtake your mind and lessen the fight within your spirit. When you allow this to happen, you hold yourself back from the blessings that await you. While storms may be pouring down in one area, the sun still shines beautifully in another. The same rings true in your life.

When you allow challenges to become stronger, you will be limited from reaching greater heights. The greater heights down the line could be points in life that you may never have imagined would come about, due to what is taking place at this moment. Nevertheless, it takes faith to stand strong against the challenges in front of you, so that you will move beyond those challenges.

Pain tends to be the foundation of the challenges that present themselves in our lives. This is because we are forced out of our comfort zones, as we are pushed beyond our normal boundaries. Pain makes us push ourselves well beyond where we normally are. With this, we are placed at points of uncertainty. When this happens, we often allow doubt to overtake our minds, and we let go of the drive that lives within our spirits. Even so, pain only lasts as long as we allow ourselves to believe that the challenges we face are too much for us. Walk through pain. Don't dwell in its lane!

When faith resides within you, it does not matter what the challenge presented to you happens to be. You will boldly take a stand against the challenge, and push yourself to gain something from the challenge. Never forget that there is a purpose behind whatever the challenge is that you are going through.

God has placed you in every situation for a reason. Where you are, where you have been, or where you will be…these are all points where God places you for a reason. Our Heavenly Father makes no mistakes when matching you to your circumstances. No matter what in your life happens to be taking place, never simply stop and quit the race. Listen to what God is saying through your situation.

For every step you take in your circumstance, God has a purpose. For every move you make in your circumstance, God has a purpose. "And we know that all things work together for the good of those who love Him, who have been called according to His purpose" (Romans 8:28 NIV). We serve a purposeful God who has purposeful blessings waiting for you. He is using what you are going through to show you what your purpose happens to be. The Lord has provided you with everything you need to face every situation that comes before you. However, it is up to you to take a faithful stand in the sand against whatever battle you are facing.

Don't embrace the "I wish" mindset. Despite what the situation you are enduring happens to be, don't step into it each time you face it with thoughts that mirror the words, "I wish I didn't have to go through this," or "I wish I could be doing something else." If God wanted you to be somewhere else, that's where you would be. If God wanted you to be doing something else, that's what you would be doing.

The way God made you and where He placed you is exactly what He meant to do. Our Heavenly Father made you fearfully and wonderfully in His image. If you needed to be taller, you would be taller. If you needed to be faster, you would be faster. If you needed to be a great singer, you would be a great singer. If you needed to be in another place, you would be in that place. Don't take any gift you have for granted. Don't take any place where you happen to be for granted.

Keep in mind that God may be using your present state of affairs to place you on a different path that is the *right* path for you. My friend, you may happen to strive to excel as a nurse. However, it may be that God is illustrating to you, through your current situation, that your true calling is in the legal field. You may be a student who needs to have great public speaking skills to exceed in your field, yet you have a significant stuttering problem. This may be God's hand at work showing you that your true calling is to be an author. God's hand never moves without a purpose.

Always step back from your situation to reflect upon what God is working to show you. Despite how difficult your circumstances are, it is not always the case that God is working to lead you down a different path. The Lord may want to bring to your realization how strongly you want to be in a certain place, or do a specific thing. Perhaps His plan is to make you hold onto what you have, or what you are working to have, even more. Speak to God for Him to reaffirm where you should be, and what you should be doing.

After reading this sentence, close your eyes and think of any frustrations that are present in your life. Despite how frustrating your situation may seem to you, think of how many people are working hard to reach your point of frustration. Nothing makes us appreciate our frustrations more than the blessings that go along with them.

If you're a parent who is frustrated with your children, think of all the people out there who are going to doctors over and over, but they still cannot conceive a child. Better yet, if you're a parent who is frustrated with your children, think of the parents crying at this very moment because of the loss of a child. If you're frustrated with being a teacher, think of all the people who are working hard to pass the teaching certification exam. However, they have not been able to pass it. If you're frustrated with being a judge, think of all the people who have completed law school, but cannot pass the bar exam.

If you're frustrated with being a surgeon, think of all the people who cannot get into medical school. If you're frustrated with your college courses, think of all the people who received letters that began with these disheartening words: *We regret to inform you that you were not admitted to our university.* On top of situations like these, think of one that generally stands out the most: If you're frustrated with your place of employment, think of all the people struggling with unemployment, especially when they have families to support financially.

Faith is a strong spiritual factor that overpowers frustration, at any point in time, all of the time. It may appear to you that each time you blink your eyes, even more tough times rush into your life, like tides of angry trouble crashing against you. Do not adopt that manner of thinking. Never let that mindset overpower you. Hold strong to the belief that the power of God is at work in your life, and His supernatural forces will bless you to conquer any circumstance that comes before you.

Our frustrations often even come from the very blessings that we asked God to receive. Think of the corporate executive who is frustrated because of the amount of paperwork that goes along with the job. Think of the principal who is frustrated because of the amount of time that must be spent with administrative duties. Both of these situations involve people who longed to have a higher blessing at one point, but became frustrated with what came along with their blessings, at a later point. Does this sound like you? Does this sound like something that has happened to you? Have you ever wanted to receive something in life, but you felt it was more than what you could bear, after you received it?

Regardless of what God brings into your life, whether it is a blessing or a point on the path to a blessing, His work is always working in your favor. Our Heavenly Father's works take place *for* you, not against you. When your faith resides in Him, your future is sunny with a certainty of success! Despite any low point where you may take one step, always keep in mind that God has an even higher step, ready and waiting to counteract that low point.

My friend, you have whatever you need for wherever you need it, at any point in time that you need it. Relax within your spirit, knowing that you have everything needed at this time to fulfill your purpose. Let your soul gain rest, not unrest. "Yes, my soul, find rest in God; my hope comes from Him" (Psalm 62:5 NIV). Allow a restful spirit within you to suppress a worrisome mindset. As time continues, if you need any further gifts to increase your blessings, God will provide you with them. At this point, you are fine with what you have, because it is what God knows that you need.

No one goes through life without troubles. We all endure times of trouble. Jesus Christ himself endured troubles. Even while writing this book, troubles have manifested in my life. Nevertheless, I have not allowed them to take hold of my life. Never let a trouble of any kind control your life. Never let any person control your life. Don't walk around with troubles on your mind. Don't let hard times hinder your spirit.

There are so many times when we see one setback as the last stage at which we may pursue the next point in our lives. Setbacks are temporary troubles that take place in all of our lives, but it is our choice of how we handle those troubles. We may choose to look beyond our troubles, knowing that God's work is taking place behind the scenes. On the other hand, we may choose to focus on the troubles in our lives at this point, and place them on center stage. Never embrace the belief that a setback on Monday will make you unable to meet a goal on Saturday.

Don't always see a bad break as the last break. God may be allowing you to fall back at one point so that you will spring up toward much higher points. It is so easy to let your focus rest upon two words: *What if?* What if I went to the other college, instead of this one? What if I chose the other career over this one? What if I accepted the other job offer, instead of this one? What if I would have had children when I could have? Just reading all of these questions, what do they all have in common? Each of them is a wonder of what could have happened. If time still permits, go for it! Don't simply live in a world of wonder. On the other hand, if time does not permit for you to pursue what you wanted to at one point in life, it is not in God's plan for it to be a part of your life.

When something is meant by the will of God for you, it will be a blessing for you. "For God's gifts and His call are irrevocable" (Romans 11:29 NIV). God's calling for your life is irrevocably present. If you are meant to be a mother, you will become a mother. If you are meant to be a father, you will become a father. If you are meant to be a teacher, you will become a teacher. If you are meant to be a doctor, you will become a doctor. If you are meant to be a preacher, you will become a preacher. Whatever it is that may not have taken place yet in your life, if it is in the will of God for it to happen, it *will* happen! If there is a past passion within you that exists for something you did not achieve, don't let the wonders of yesterday hinder you today and delay you tomorrow.

"When you carry the weight of yesterday, it will ruin the power and progress of tomorrow."
—Dr. Tony Evans

Pursue your past passion if you can, but let go of it if you can't. Don't live in the past. Don't spend all of your time looking in the rearview mirror when your spirit needs to look through the windshield. Focus on the present. Allow your proper focus to make you excel in the here and now, and let that success continue in the future. If wondering about the past is a problem for you, take the time to reflect upon it. Pray to God for His guiding actions. Time of reflection about your circumstances serves as a calm in the storm of your situation.

After taking the time to reflect, one of two things will happen. God will show you that His plan is for you to let go of what you once pursued, or He will open your eyes as to what can be done to allow you to achieve your goal. If you once wanted to have children, but your age now serves as a hindrance to that happening, God may show you, after your time of reflection, that you should adopt children. You may serve as the well-needed parent that some child out there needs. If your stuttering problem hinders your public speaking, God's plan may be for you to sing. God has given you a gift of some sort. Embrace that gift, and use it to allow you to let go of the fumbles of your past.

Keep your eyes focused upon what is in front of you. Don't turn to look back at what is behind you. When houses are built, they generally do not come with only one door. Why is that? It is because there is more than one way to enter and exit. Just because one way does not work does not mean that *another* way will not. On top of that, just because one way does not work does not mean that *no* way will work. If one way of achieving a goal did not work in your past, don't simply hang your head in defeat. Look beyond that to find a better way to reach your goal. Look beyond hard times, and look toward better times.

Too often, we allow challenges to make us give up on things that could lead us to be our best. We permit a fear of failure to make us close the door on a dream. We allow the doubt of whether or not we "have what it takes" to become what makes us give up on our dreams. Why do we often do this? It is so that others don't get a new perception of us, if we fail.

My friend, the views that others have of you are not what make you who you are. Why are you focusing so much of your attention on other people? Why are you allowing others to have so much of your time and energy? Why are you working so hard to impress others, instead of working hard to be the best **YOU** that **YOU** can be?

Don't ever give up on something because of what others may think of you. My friend, don't let a challenge at one point make you think that you will never reach greater heights at another point. When you keep the faith, you allow the passion within you to motivate you to take the actions that you need to take. This allows you to move forward to the points where you need to be.

You are who you are, despite where you are. The place where you are now does not define you. Our Heavenly Father defines you. He is the *ultimate* dictionary. God has you where you are for a reason. When all is said and done, where you are and where you have been will lead you to more superior times ahead. Being at a certain place in life may make it seem like you will never succeed. My friend, it is not about your location, but your motivation. Your motivation to move forward to better times ahead stirs up your faith, and makes it stronger. The way you see your situation, the approach you take to your situation, and the way you move through your situation guides you to points of triumph.

> **"It's not about the cards you're dealt, but how you play the hand."**
>
> — **Randy Pausch**

There are so many times when we embrace the idea that our lives are about what happens to us, rather than our reactions from what happens. Most of the outcomes of situations in our lives depend upon our reactions to them.

> **"Life is ten percent what happens to you and ninety percent how you respond to it."**
> **— Lou Holtz**

What if I happened to be one of the best workers at a plant for the last twenty years, only to walk in and be told, on a random day, that my "services are no longer needed?" One of two things could happen. I could react to the situation in a negative fashion that makes me move even lower in life, or I could allow my faith to push me to even greater heights ahead.

From a standpoint of faith, being laid off may provide me with the opportunity to finally open my own million-dollar business, using the knowledge and skills that I had been holding back for many years. From a standpoint of frustration, this situation could lead me to grasp the belief that I don't have what it takes to be a worker for anyone. With this, I might embrace the belief that I should stop working hard altogether, because I will never be appreciated. As such, I might become highly impoverished, wondering where my next meal would come from each day.

Regardless of what takes place in your life, keep your head up! In the first previous example, God moved the person from being laid off to becoming a million-dollar business owner. While God was showing the person that working for someone else was not in His plan in both examples, the person's reactions showed two different outcomes of the situation. By following faith, the person was shown that becoming the owner of a million-dollar business was the ultimate plan for the individual. By giving into frustration, the person became very poor, both financially and spiritually. Despite your situation, keep working hard and keep the faith. By doing this, your season of success will come. "Sluggards do not plow in season; so, at harvest time they look but find nothing" (Proverbs 20:4 NIV).

Let your times of frustration serve as your motivation. I cannot say enough that these times in life are only temporary periods. Your times of frustration are simply places on the map of your life, which you will walk through, not permanent destinations. During the years of my childhood, my mother would kneel and pray with me each night before going to bed. Before beginning our silent prayers, we would recite *Psalm 23* aloud, in order to serve as a connection between a biblical scripture and our personal prayers. Each time I think about my times of frustration, I keep this scripture in mind, as I remind myself that better times are ahead for me. "Yea, though I walk through the valley of the shadow of death, I will fear no evil: for thou art with me; thy rod and thy staff they comfort me" (Psalm 23:4 KJV). Hold strong to your faith that the Lord is allowing your times of frustration to be the soil that will allow you to blossom into successful times ahead.

A time of frustration has a time of arrival that God has scheduled to arrive in your life. Even so, it also has a time that God has scheduled for it to depart from your life. Your frustrations may appear to be stagnant points in your life, but God always has a reason for allowing that delay to be present. Take the time to see what God is showing you, as He allows the frustrations that you are facing to be present in your life. Close your natural eyes and look through the eyes of faith to see what God wants you to see. Our Heavenly Father never leaves you by yourself in any situation. He is always there for you. "God is our refuge and strength, a very present help in trouble" (Psalm 46:1 KJV).

There is never a time in your life when God allows a time of frustration, a time of apparent discouragement, to be present without a purpose. See things through the eyes of faith so that you will know why your frustration exists. Let every second of frustration be counteracted by a higher point of motivation. Don't be overcome with discouragement, but be inspired by encouragement.

Times of frustration are like the dark points of the midnight hour. Nevertheless, I cannot encourage you enough to call on Jesus in the midnight hour of your problems, because there is no storm that He cannot calm.

When it seems like there is no way for you to find a way that will lead you to better times, call on Jesus every time, at any time, all of the time!

It may feel as if the more you fight to get away from a frustrating situation, the more you are drawn back to it. Perhaps God is showing you that it is not in His plan for you to be removed from that situation. His plan may be to make the crooked places, at that very point, straight for you. As you look at your situation through the eyes of faith, you may see that God is stretching your strength right where you are, so that you will accomplish great things.

Think of a young man who strongly dislikes the amount of time that being in college appears to take away from his life, along with having to work to pay for college. God may not let him out of his situation because it is in God's plan for the young man to one day become a world-renowned researcher who finds a cure for cancer.

Think of a young lady who wants to move beyond law school to a different career path, but each time she attempts to pursue a different career, she is led back to law school. She might pursue a career as an engineer, only to be led back to law. She might pursue a career as a teacher, only to be led back to law. She might pursue a career as a pharmacist, only to be led back to law. This may be happening because it is in God's plan for her to someday become a very distinguished attorney who has her client found not guilty, instead of facing the death penalty. Although it may appear to an outsider looking in that the young lady has made many mistakes with her career choices, these were not mistakes. These points in her life have simply served as manifestations of the foundation of her true place as an attorney.

Too often in life we allow ourselves to take on the belief, in certain circumstances, that darkness is always what we see when we look around. That is not true. Just as there are periods of daylight, there must also be periods of darkness. Just as there are periods of sunlight, there must also be periods of rainfall. Just as there are periods of springtime, there must also be periods of fall. Just as there are periods of summertime, there must also be periods of winter. These are all cycles. If one cycle did not happen, we would not have the appreciation of another.

My friend, there are a high number of times when it appears that we have troubles that will not let go of our lives. It tends to appear that when we open our eyes, we are faced with trouble. When we sit up in bed, we are faced with trouble. When we step outside, we are faced with trouble. It may seem like no matter what we do, we are faced with trouble. In spite of this, never let times of trouble overtake you. "The righteous person may have many troubles, but the LORD delivers him from them all" (Psalm 34:19 NIV).

It does not matter what troubles you may be facing, close your natural eyes and open your eyes of faith to look at the troubles, in order to see that blessings will come from them. Although you may have troubles at this point in your life from the time you open your eyes to the time you close them, be thankful that you *can* open your eyes. While you may have troubles from the time you sit up in bed to the time that you lie down, be thankful that you *can* sit up in bed. Despite the reality that you may be faced with troubles from the point you step outside, be thankful that you *can* step outside. Regardless of the troubles that may exist in your life, find some way to be thankful to the Lord. Give Him praise throughout the day. When your praise goes up to the Lord, blessings come down to you. When your blessings come down, you move to higher ground.

Moving forward in life often seems like one of the most difficult tasks that there could be. It often seems like the light is green for everyone else, but it turns red for you. As we see others progress, and we simply appear to remain in the very place where we are, we tend to want to give up. Adding to this, as we see others progress and we appear to digress, this makes us want to give up even more than we already did when our troubles first came. My friend, God always has a red light in place at the right time. Please also remember that God allows you to turn right on red, unless His signs say otherwise.

As we travel down the road of life, we see so many things. A red light tends to anger us, while a green light tends to bring us happiness. Even so, life also brings about yellow lights onto our paths, which may cause points of confusion. A yellow light does one of two things. It makes us slow down, or it encourages us to speed up. However, so many of us often become confused when we see a yellow light. We have a habit of mistaking a yellow light for either red or green. Instead of yielding, we keep going at the same pace because we see no difference between the green and yellow lights. On the other hand, instead of yielding, we stop, because we see no difference between the yellow and red lights. This is all the more reason why we must listen to the Lord, so that we may see things according to His will. As we listen to His guidance, we move as He desires for us to move, in the timing that He wants us to move.

God may tell us to stop, slow down, speed up, or keep going at the same pace. However, He is always telling us to do something. It is up to us to listen to what the Lord is saying. When we listen to the Lord and move according to His will, it does not matter how angrily the tides of trouble violently move upon us. He will bring about a calm in the storm. Think of the last time you rushed into making a decision that turned out the opposite way of what you thought it would. Did it turn out better than you anticipated, or did it turn out worse? When things happen for the better as you proceed quickly, this shows that the light turned yellow as you correctly sped up on your path. At the same time, when things happen worse than expected when you sped up, this tends to be because your speed was not on God's accord.

Despite how things have happened in your life, good or bad, God is *still* great! Just because something did not turn out well yesterday does not mean He cannot make it turn out well today. While things may appear to be going every way but the right way today, this does not mean that God will not steer you to a better point tomorrow. The wrong turn today may be the right turn tomorrow. Sometimes it takes traveling in a different direction to reach your destination, but in a better way. When God makes us move, remember that we should move with faith. As we move with faith, God shifts us in the right direction.

Faith sparks a self-fulfilling prophecy. Having faith ensures that you will not fall to failure, but stand strongly with success. You must have a spirit of faith that illuminates through you, as you face the challenges of life. The hope that dwells within you must shine through the eyes of your faith; as you look adversity right in the eye, smile with confidence that triumph will be in your favor.

The eyes of faith are not like the eyes of man. My friend, the eyes of faith are unique in the sense that they put fear aside, and look up to God for guidance toward victory. On the other hand, the eyes of man see things exactly how they are, in the clear, plain space. If your situation *only* looks like you will not move to a better point, you know that the eyes of man are seeing the situation. Regardless of how the situation looks to man, the power of God always has the final say over the situation. Knowing this, the eyes of faith clearly see victory from all sides, because they do not look toward the blind spot of fear that tempts you to take your eyes off the prize of victory. By viewing your life through the eyes of faith, you are able to see the power of God at work. When the power of God is at work, it does not matter how strongly the situation may seem to be against you. God always allows things to turn out well for you.

As you see life through the eyes of faith, you are able to look ahead. Faith lets you focus on what is ahead of you, not dwell on what is behind you. It does not matter what has taken place in your past. If it was five seconds ago or five years ago, it has *already* happened. Concentrate on what is taking place now. Let your focus rest upon how you can use the here and now to make things better in the future. Keep the faith! Stay in faith! Preserve your faith!

When faith lives within you, favor comes to you. It does not matter if a thousand people have said "no," all it takes is the favor of God to be blessed to have the *right* person to say "yes."

There are so many times in life when we talk ourselves out of working toward finally hearing the "yes" that we know deep down that we have what it takes to hear. Too often, we are so quick to see things how they look to man, and then we see ourselves as not "having what it takes" as a result. My friend, don't put yourself down any longer. Don't see yourself below anyone else. Stop having negative, pessimistic thoughts. See the glass half full, not half empty. You have what it takes to be just as successful as anyone else!

Think of what this quote asks:

"What great thing would you attempt if you knew you could not fail?"

—**Robert H. Schuller**

So many great things tend to rush to mind when we reflect upon what could happen in our lives, what we could be, or what we could do. I want you to try something that I am highly confident will help you. Close your eyes for a moment. Listen to the total, relaxing silence around you. Picture the one thing that you want to do, to be, or to have. Speak these words to yourself: *I can do it! I can be it! I can have it!*

Words are so powerful. We often don't realize that when we take the time to speak them, we are taking the time to speak them into existence. Instead of giving ourselves the slightest grain of confidence, we often allow doubts and worries to make us accept failure, instead of continuing the fight. My friend, please don't let this be what you do. When you wake up in the morning, speak these words into existence: *I am blessed! Regardless what takes place today, the favor of God will still rain down upon me!*

Believe, every day, that you have what it takes to reach excellence. Affirm, every morning, that excellence is on your path. Announce, every afternoon, that greatness is coming to you. Declare, every evening, that victory is headed your way. When you allow your words to be positive, you will embrace a positive mindset. With a positive mindset, you will have a faithful spirit. By having a spirit of faith, you are able to overcome the natural and see the supernatural taking place in your life. Words have a calming effect upon any storm of life, when they are delivered in a positive fashion. No matter what you may be facing, always find something positive about the situation. Speak out about the positive points that exist for you, and allow them to rise above the negative points.

Regardless of your set of circumstances, acknowledge the excellence of God! It may seem to the natural eye that there is no way that you will overcome what you are facing. Perhaps you are a cancer patient who has been told she will not live beyond the next five months. You may conceivably be an innocent man who has been sentenced to time in prison for a crime he did not commit. Perchance you may even be the parent of a child who is unlikely to be admitted to a college, even though your child has what it takes to become a graduate of that college. Although any of these situations, or some of the like, may mirror your set of circumstances, never hang your head in defeat!

I cannot emphasize enough that you must look through the eyes of faith to show your acknowledgement of the power of God to be triumphant over your challenges. Regardless of what man has said, you have what it takes to overcome any situation through your trust in God. "Trust in the Lord with all thine heart; and lean not unto thine own understanding. In all thy ways acknowledge Him, and He shall direct thy paths" (Proverbs 3:5-6 KJV). When God is acknowledged, His supernatural hand overpowers the natural problems we may face in the blink of an eye.

By acknowledging God for who He is, we show our trust in Him. When we rightfully acknowledge our Heavenly Father, we acknowledge our trust in Him. When our trust and acknowledgment are given to God, all things are possible. "Those who trust in the Lord are like Mount Zion, which cannot be shaken but endures forever" (Psalm 125:1 NIV). Trust in the Lord lessens your doubts and strengthens your faith. With faith, hope floats on worry, and makes worry cease. No matter what your situation happens to be, remember that you have the blood of excellence of our Heavenly Father flowing through your veins! Let this simple, yet significant thought make you wash aside any and every worry that may attempt to manifest itself in your mind.

Worrying is an action that consumes today with apprehensions about tomorrow, and unrest about yesterday, which makes you not truly enjoy today. How can you believe that God will bring about a better tomorrow if you don't believe that He can handle today? In the game of life, you cannot play tomorrow's game before you play the one today. No matter how much you want to get to your next stage in life, you have got to handle today before you can handle tomorrow. Push aside worry and embrace an expectance of favor. When the favor of God comes upon you, mountains are moved, no matter how big or small. "For his anger lasts only a moment, but his favor lasts a lifetime; weeping may stay for the night, but rejoicing comes in the morning" (Psalm 30:5 NIV).

Instead of worrying about what may happen tomorrow, enjoy the current moments of today! Regardless how good, bad, or in between today happens to be, find something about today to enjoy! It is up to you to live one day at a time. This will allow you to have a love for life, no matter if times are bursting with happiness, or flaming with frustration.

"Life lived for tomorrow will always be just a day away from being realized."
—Leo Buscaglia

Don't let all your desires rest upon tomorrow. Rejoice upon the greatness that is present today!

Chapter Three

VICTORY RESIDES IN BELIEF

Do you believe you *can* do it? Do you believe you *will* do it? Do you believe you have what it takes? Questions like these often enter our minds when we face challenges associated with the pursuit of our goals. No matter if our goals simply require us to take a small step or a giant leap, there is often something that attempts to place itself on our minds or within our spirits to hold us back. Regardless what we have the potential to do, or what we have the potential to become, doubt does its best to drive us back from our best.

One problem tends to exist on the edge of victory and defeat: *belief.* This is a small, yet giant aspect of the outcomes of life's situations. Belief is a strong factor in the foundation of any kind of victory. My friend, you have what it takes to be a victor of your challenges, not a victim. It does not matter how many people have told you that you do not have what it takes to conquer your dreams. Do not listen to them. There is nothing that you cannot do when you believe that you can do it. Why is that? It is because you have faith when you believe. When you believe, substance is given to your hope. When you believe, evidence is brought forth to what you do not see. When you believe, there is no victory that you cannot achieve.

A lack of belief is not only a hurtful factor upon the success of one person, but it can also become a hurtful factor upon the success of a massive segment of the population. As I stepped back to look at the lack of achievement of individuals in certain places, I was inspired to reach out to young people in some of those places who are often overlooked in society. I have been blessed to have the opportunity to mentor many young people in my efforts to keep them on the right track in life. The youth who I mentor are often looked down upon in society, and regarded as being "at-risk." These are individuals who are "statistically" seen as high school dropouts, as well as being viewed as "likely" to have "many run-ins" with the law.

The driving force as to why these young people are often seen by others in such a negative light is their socio-economic status. One of my mentees once stopped me and asked for my opinion about his future. He resonated these touching words to me: "A mean man told me the other day that "your kind" will never make it in life. Get ready to be a failure, because that is what is calling your name! He's not the first person to say something like this to me. Do you think I will be a failure?" As I listened to what he asked me, I could tell that he was truly on the edge of giving up on himself. Although this young man was more than capable to have a victorious future with a successful career, one word clearly came to mind for me as to what was holding him back from victory: *belief*.

In every moment of the day, our beliefs are at work. When we are told by many others that we will succeed, the belief of success in our future takes root. On the other hand, when we are told by many others that failure is in our future, belief often begins to lack in our lives. As we sit awaiting a job interview, we may see another individual who is going in for an interview before us for the same job. This person may strike up a conversation with us, and even allow us to see his or her resume. The person's work history may appear so amazing that it makes us embrace the belief that we are too average to get the job, which makes us put forth less effort during the interview than we normally would. However, it may not be that the boss is looking for someone with a great resume. The boss may want someone who is new to the field. Even so, we must still put forth our best effort to show that we are the right choice. Knowing this, your belief cannot be a wavering factor. It must stand strong, regardless of what surrounds it.

Belief is the guiding principle behind any victory. Whatever you believe you will become, this is what you will eventually become. Whatever you believe you do not have what it takes to become, you will not become. My friend, the good news for you is that *you* choose what you believe. If you want to have a certain career, you get to believe that you will be a part of that career. If you want to beat a disease, you get to believe you will beat the disease. When you walk throughout the day thinking, "I believe I can do this" and "I believe this will happen," you are setting yourself up in the right place to achieve victory. By believing you will achieve victory, you are placing yourself on the right path for victory to come to you.

By having such strong power exist behind our beliefs, we must be very careful with what we believe. Don't ever invite defeat into your life with the wrong belief. Imagine if you were to go into a hospital saying, "I believe these might be my final days." What do you think could be very likely to happen? You might just be in the final days of your life. Why is this? It is because you are inviting the final days of your life to take place.

Don't think that God isn't listening to what you have to say. Whether it is aloud or in your mind, God is listening to you. How can you say that you want something to happen, but then have thoughts expressing the belief that it will never occur? How can you want a blessing so badly, but have doubtful beliefs that follow that desire? Please keep in mind that God is always listening to you. Having this in mind, it is important to pray. Through prayer, you invite God to listen to your open spirit with a humble heart so that His power will go to work through your beliefs.

Prayer is an important part of your beliefs. How often do you pray, but lack belief behind your prayers for you to receive your blessings? My friend, you cannot just ask God to bless you. You must first *believe* that He will bless you, in order for you to see your blessings come to life. "But when you ask, you must believe and not doubt, because the one who doubts is like a wave of the sea, blown and tossed by the wind" (James 1:6 NIV). God is not limited in His power. With this in mind, don't limit your blessings by lacking belief. Don't limit yourself through doubt. No blessing is too much for God to give, and no blessing is too big for you to receive. "And all things, whatsoever ye shall ask in prayer, believing, ye shall receive" (Matthew 21:22 KJV).

Declare by faith: *My victory is coming!* Embrace the belief: *My victory is coming!* Pronounce with passion: *My victory is coming!* By allowing yourself to take hold of this new mindset of confidence, your faith will move you into victorious grounding. Grasp a mindset of nothing being impossible for you. Embrace a spirit of hope. Allow substance to come forth to your faith. See how far the water in your glass happens to be from the top of the glass, not how close it is to the bottom of the glass.

Despite how difficult the days of your life may seem, don't look down. Look your challenges straight in the eye with confidence, knowing that victory is on its way into your life. Show that you believe you will succeed by stepping out on faith. Take the risks you need to take to succeed.

Perhaps you have been a devoted worker at a company for many years, but it has been in the back of your mind for a long period of time to become a business owner. On one hand, having a steady job that has a secure paycheck coming each month may seem like the best thing for you. On the other hand, taking the risk to set aside a high amount of your upcoming paychecks to invest toward your own company may be the right path for you to follow. While earning thirty thousand dollars a year might be a "secure" salary, taking the risk to become a business owner may bring forth thirty million dollars a year. The risk that you may need to take has the potential to illustrate itself as a testimony of what your beliefs are able to bring about in your life.

Don't simply take actions related to what the natural eye shows you will happen, or will not happen. Strongly step toward what your beliefs speak into existence. Don't limit yourself. We serve a limitless Lord. Regardless what your victory happens to be, believe that it will happen. Hold strong to the belief that your victory will come to pass. If you have an addiction to drugs, embrace the belief that you will overcome your addiction. If you are fighting a disease, hold strong to the belief that you will win the battle against the disease. If you are passionately searching for employment, accept the belief that God will place you in the right place of employment at the right time. If you are working to become a business owner, take hold of the belief that you will one day become the owner of one of the most financially prosperous businesses in history. In order to be a winner, you must first *believe* that you are a winner. In order to have victory, you must accept yourself as a victor.

Close your eyes for a moment. Envision what it is that you are facing at this very moment that you are striving to achieve. Take the next 60 seconds to see yourself, in your mind, reaching that goal at this exact point in time. How did that reflection make you feel? What was it like to see yourself being successful? What was it like for you to see yourself wearing the shoes of victory? Being able to see yourself achieving a goal is the starting point of victory. To believe it, you must see it. To achieve it, you must first believe it.

Belief is what starts a blessing. When you believe, you are not asking for a favor from man. Your belief lays the foundation for your faith to open the door for you to achieve greatness, because you then have limitless confidence. To be a winner, you must have the attitude of a winner.

There are so many times when people talk about sports, and how there is no way that one team will ever win over another. Nevertheless, there are also many times when they are mesmerized by how the underdog of the situation comes out on top. Times like these are when fans are at a loss of words by how the "worse" team beats the "better" team. With this having recently happened with the football team of my college alma mater winning against one of our highest sports rivals, I was inspired to see this as a real-life analogy. "On paper" something could be impossible. There is no way that it could happen. You might as well not even take one step toward it becoming a reality, according to what's "on paper." Even so, that's why they play the game. The same certainly rings true in real life. While "on paper" your victory will never occur, believing that you have what it takes tends to overpower what is against you "on paper."

Being the underdog of a situation tends to incline us to naturally lean toward embracing defeat, before we even put forth the smallest magnitude of effort. The same rings especially true after we have given the situation a vast amount of effort. I cannot say enough about how much difficulties put us to the test. However, simply being tested does not automatically lead to failure. After we stop running from the test and take the test, we may happen to see that the test is what is being used to move us to even greater heights, both literally and figuratively.

My friend, I have no idea what the test happens to be in your life. While I'm unaware of what the test happens to be that is presenting itself to you, I am aware that you have what it takes to excel against that test. Too often, we allow our past poor test performance to bring about negative views of the outcome of our present test to seep into our minds, and weaken the faith within our spirits. Nonetheless, to move to greater heights, you must forget about poor outcomes of the past. In order to turn to a new page, you must let go of the previous page.

As you let go of yesterday, you are able to enjoy today. You are able to move toward a better future with ease. Releasing the hold that the past has upon you shows that the belief for your victorious times ahead resides within you. By not allowing the problems of your past to be a detriment to you today, you are able to gain the satisfaction of victory on any day, good or bad. In the midnight hour, God will devour all the demons that try to hold you down. Just keep the faith! When faith lives within you, God makes yesterday's impossibilities become today's realities. Through your faith, belief in the great times ahead of you will bring those great times to you.

Belief is always a strong factor in the receipt of blessings. There is nothing that you cannot achieve when you first believe that you can achieve it. At the same time, God's timing for our blessings not always being in correlation with our timing tends to have a strong reason behind it. We often long for the satisfaction of our blessings. In spite of that, as much as we long for satisfaction, we often do not know what it is that will truly bring us satisfaction. This tends to be a reason why we have not received the blessings that we want. God wants us to truly understand what we are blessed with when we are blessed.

Many times, people find it so hard to wait on a blessing. They want it here and now, no other way. These individuals have an inability to delay gratification. Nevertheless, God does not work this way. He wants us to appreciate what He gives us. The Lord wants us to open our hands with thankfulness, as we receive our blessings. He wants us to accept the gifts He gives us, with humble hearts. Waiting on our Heavenly Father with faith stirred up within our spirits, and holding strong to a mindset of belief, leads us to the receipt of our blessings. "But they that wait upon the LORD shall renew their strength; they shall mount up with wings as eagles; they shall run, and not be weary; and they shall walk, and not faint" (Isaiah 40:31 KJV). When you wait on our Father to do His work, you are empowered with greatness. When you wait on our Father to do His work, you are lifted up with power. When you wait on our Father to do His work, you rise into victory.

Through your belief in God's power to bless you, faith becomes a central part of your spirit. When your faith rests upon God's power, you embrace a spirit of optimism. When you take hold of the belief that God will show His power in your life on your behalf, you embrace a spirit of optimism. Having optimism within your spirit brings about positive outcomes in your life, because you are able to spiritually stand your ground against obstacles. Optimistic behavior leads you into prosperous territory, as the favor of God rains down upon you with blessings. With optimism at your forefront, you are inspired to put forth zestful actions that make you spring forward into victory. It is not in the plan for you to sit back and do nothing, in order for you to be blessed. Actions must be taken on your part for you to move forward.

> **"Don't sit down and wait for opportunities to come. Get up and make them!"**
> —Madam C.J. Walker

My friend, as much as you want something to happen, you must still take a stand and put action behind your desires. In order to move yourself from the status quo, you must be willing to do something to move yourself from the status quo. Belief goes along with action. Faith goes along with action. Favor is given as a result of action. Mercy is shown as a result of action. "For as the body without the spirit is dead, so faith without works is dead also" (James 2:26 KJV). Our faith is truly shown through our actions. When we are not afraid to take a stand for something in which we believe, we illustrate our faith.

Our actions, or lack thereof, tend to be a reflection of how relaxed we are in a particular situation. We generally move in a much more relaxed manner, when we know where we are going. When we know where we are going, it makes a big difference. Even as we endure the storms of life, we still move about in a more relaxed, prosperous manner... when we know where we are going.

I want you to see this for yourself. Close your eyes for a moment. Think of the last time you were driving in an area with which you were familiar. Paint a mental picture in your mind of your body language as you drove. How were you sitting? Was it in a more relaxed fashion, or a more uptight fashion? How were you holding the steering wheel? Were your hands more at ease, or were your hands tightly gripping the steering wheel?

When you know where you are going, you can even move about in darkness with ease and relaxation, because there is a light to your travel. Picture the last time you were walking around your house with the lights off. Why were you able to walk at your regular pace without problems? Why was there ease instead of tension within you as you traveled? Why did you not need the physical lights to be on for you to successfully move from one point to another? It is because you knew where you were going. By knowing where you are going, there is a light that shines on your behalf, which takes away the need for the light of man.

Too often, we *know of* where we are going, but we don't *know* where we are going. Picture it as sunlight shining on your path, but fog being impressed upon it, at the same time. While sunlight is shining in situations such as these, fog still exists. Being aware of this, the truth remains that it is much easier when you know where you are going, in order to arrive where you desire to be. In times when you are uncertain of where you are going, don't just stop and give up. Pray to God for direction.

Embrace the realization that you must know the Lord, in order for you to reach your destination of victory. When you *know of* the Lord, you are hindering yourself from receiving the guidance of His hand. You are holding yourself back from receiving His wonders of excellence in your life. However, when you *know* the Lord, He leads your every step and guides you with His grace.

Let the hand of God direct your movement. Our Heavenly Father will give you traveling grace during whatever storms that life places upon you as you move. God will not only guide you to your destination, but He will also lead you each step of the way, when you follow Him. The most maturing times of our faith tend to be when we don't know where we are going. *Why is this?* It is because this is when we truly step aside and let God do His work. It is at these times when we put down our pencil and paper from unprosperous attempts to take notes on what we did not understand. Then, we just watch God's work in action, so that we can imitate His greatness through our actions.

Our belief in the power of God at work in our lives is what allows us to trust in His work. We are able to know where we are going, because our connection with God leads Him to let our belief show us where we are going. Belief makes us aware of our destination. Faith keeps us relaxed as we advance toward our destination. When we have belief and faith as the guiding factors on the map of reaching our goals, we are able to take the actions we need to take, and move toward our goals with ease.

Belief and faith are often two lacking factors, when it comes to why we don't achieve our goals. There are so many times that we don't pursue something, because we are afraid of the outcome. At times, when we are confident that we will not be placed on the path of our truly desired destination, but we simply want to say, "I tried," for an ease of mind, we will pursue our goals. However, we do not believe we have what it takes to achieve those goals. With this, we tend to pursue opportunities the wrong way, and we won't actually move toward them.

Think of a woman who spent a large amount of her childhood in hospital waiting rooms, due to her father's health troubles. While many of her friends had the leisure to simply sit at home, complaining about the television shows that were on at particular times, she was with her family, wondering if the medical staff would come out and say that her father was no longer alive. Although this could have had an intensely negative psychological impact on her life, it did the opposite. These experiences stirred up a strong desire within her to become a doctor. Despite this, one bad academic experience led her to believe that she did not have what it took to become a doctor, let alone be a doctor for many years to come. As a result, she turned her back on her dream. Years later, she finally felt the need to reach back and see if she really did have what it took to be a doctor. She soon found that not only did she have what it took to become one, she had what it took to be a great one!

Have you ever met a person who started down a path to become something in life that they truly wanted to be, but they gave up because they accepted the belief that they "don't have what it takes?" You may have asked them, "Well, if you love *that* so much, then why are you doing *this*?" That question has the tendency to stir up a totally different, often heated conversation, all because the person still wants to be what they pursued at one point in life. However, this person did not believe they could actually succeed in that career.

There are so many situations where we are scared to step into unfamiliar territory; this is because we don't feel like we have what it takes to succeed in that unfamiliar territory. To overcome this, we must be willing to take risks. We can't be afraid of failure. Just remember that it is not about the seemingly failing set of circumstances, but your reaction to them that matters.

> "Failure is simply the opportunity to begin again more intelligently."
>
> —Henry Ford

When you take a fall in life, what will be your reaction to the set of circumstances? Will you work to make yourself better as a result of the situation, or will you give up altogether?

Nothing becomes a true failure, until you let it get the best of you. A technical difficulty in life may cause your situation to pause, but that does not mean it will stop. In every setback, there is a lesson to be learned. It is what you carry away from the situation that matters. The biggest lesson to carry away from the outcome of any set of circumstances, good or bad, is that we gain victory because of our belief that it will come. With our belief that victory will come, we put forth faithful actions to bring about the right opportunities in our lives. Along with our actions and beliefs, comes prayer. When we call on Jesus, there is nothing that we are not able to achieve.

Through our beliefs, we stop worry from getting the best of us. Worrying is not an action that removes the days to come of their setbacks, but it does take away the good times of today. When you fill your mind with thoughts of mediocrity, failure, and uncertainty, your life will be filled with mediocrity, failure, and uncertainty. A victor does not just settle for being "satisfactory" or "just okay." A victor is not just an "acceptable" person. This individual is a person who has a mindset of purposeful proficiency, and strives to exceed even the most excellent person in the domain where his or her dream happens to be. Embracing qualities, such as these, makes you triumphantly reach your goals. You must embody belief through a purposeful pursuit of your passion, and have faith that confidently stands behind that passion, in order for you to reach victory.

As long as you are content with settling for a stagnant position of mediocrity, you will be in a state of mediocrity. However, when you embellish your mind with thoughts of success and victory, you will have a life bursting with success and victory. You are able to surpass adversity by the grace of God, so do not spend your time worrying about future outcomes. Instead, spend your time being confident and having faith that God will move mightily in your life, on your behalf! Just remember that God will bless you to overcome whatever adversities that life may bestow upon you. In order for you to receive your blessings, you must have faith in Him! The next time thoughts of worry attempt to overshadow your faith, just pray the words of this well-known scripture: "Lord, I believe; help my unbelief!" (Mark 9:24 NKJV).

Place faith at your forefront, and let the belief that victory is ahead of you immerse within you. By believing that victory will be our end result, we pray, instead of worrying. Prayer and worry are mutually exclusive. The two cannot take place at the same time. If you are praying, but still worrying, you are not *really* praying. This is because asking something of God rests upon the knowledge that He will grant it.

On the other hand, prayer and faith are not mutually exclusive. It takes devotion to achieve success, and faith in God to move in your life, in order to persevere against adversity during the troublesome times of life. Do not let the frustrations of life overshadow your belief in what prayer will do in your life, when it has faith behind it. Moreover, you must realize that when you have faith, there is nothing that may take place in your life that will permanently stop you from achieving victory in whatever it is that you are pursuing. "No weapon that is formed against thee shall prosper" (Isaiah 54:17 KJV).

There are times in life when we become torn between whether to give up, or to endure the struggle toward victory. Even so, when you believe in God to work it out, your victory will come about, despite any doubt! Regardless of having to endure halting hard times, your faith in the Lord is what will see you through them. Despite the tides of trouble boldly fighting against you, faith is what brings God forth to calm those troublesome tides, and serve as the bridge that will take you across troubles of any magnitude.

No matter what the challenge is that stands before you, just rest assured that God knows what to do. Despite what you may be going through, just rest assured that God will certainly see you through. While the tides of trouble may presently face you, faith makes those tides turn in your favor. Though the tides of trouble may be getting high, faith will bring you to a triumph as high as the sky. Your faith is the predecessor to receiving His favor in any situation. Once you have God's favor, there is no troublesome circumstance that you cannot overcome! Hold strong to the belief that victory is on its way to you! Hold strong to the belief that the trumpet of triumph will soon sound, when you reach your destination!

When belief dwells within your spirit, you realize that although stumbling blocks may come about on the road to success, there is no obstacle that will prosper against you, as long as you put God first. There is no obstacle that you cannot conquer through God. "Nay, in all these things we are more than conquerors through Him that loved us" (Romans 8:37 KJV).

There are so many times when we don't see that we have what it takes to be victors of a set of circumstances, because we don't step back from the situation to see the victor within us. Just think of being in your house for the majority of the day, without going outside. Now, picture yourself going outside, and then coming back inside. When you come back inside, you may notice a nice smell that had simply become unnoticeable to you. This is likely because it is around you so much that you don't take the time to pay it any attention. The smell would be something of second nature to you that you'd take for granted.

My friend, when you have what you need to have, don't overlook it. When you are very used to what you have, don't overlook it. Don't disregard the great traits that you have that will lead you to blessings. Recognize the greatness that you have within you. Identify the greatness within you. Let the greatness within you radiate itself throughout your life.

God does not give us greatness without a reason, and He does not want the greatness within our spirits to become malnourished. He wants us to know that He has not placed us where we are, without a purpose. There are lessons being taught here. There are lessons to be learned here. The lessons that God is bringing forth to us are providing our greatness with the nourishment that it needs. Nevertheless, it is up to us to let the belief within us steer us to victory.

To reach victory, you must realize that the cause and cure of your obstacles cannot be one in the same. The cause of your obstacles may make you weak, but the cure is your faith in the Lord, which makes you strong. You must accept the winning mindset that God has at your spiritual forefront, which leads and guides you on each step to the pursuit of your goals.

Too often, we harp upon a few points of a situation to the extent that we stop ourselves from reaching our true potential. Do not concentrate on the minor details of a bad situation. Instead, see the big picture. You cannot allow the setbacks of life to deter you from achieving victory. After all, a football player does not harp upon one bad play in the game, because it is only a minor detail. He focuses on the end result of the game, which is the big picture. While a wide receiver may have dropped a pass in the game, he still has to concentrate on winning the game in order to beat the opponent. The player cannot be a part of a victory, if he lets one pitfall stop him. While the dropped pass may have ruined one play, it could then inspire the player to make a touchdown in the next play. In addition, this touchdown could mean the difference between winning the game, or having a loss that should not have come.

No matter what you are facing, belief has the power to strengthen you to overcome adversity and bring forth victory. Women often face many obstacles in life that men do not. Even so, this reality does not stop a high number of women from reaching the goals that they have the desire to attain. Whether the issue involves the right to vote, or holding the same job titles as men, the strong fight in the spirit of women has brought, and is still bringing a balance between men and women. Why it that? Belief is the central reason. With belief comes faith, and with faith comes action.

For our faith to allow us to flourish, our belief must first place our eyes in the right direction, so that we will see and follow victory. Where are your eyes looking? Are your eyes looking up to God for guidance, or down to the ground with doubt? Are your eyes looking forward without limits to victory, or backward at what could lead you to defeat? Without the belief that you have what it takes to achieve victory, victory will not be on your schedule.

> **"In order to succeed, we must first believe we can."**
> **—Michael Korda**

Belief makes you break barriers. Belief makes you dare to dream of the achievement of excellence, in whatever you pursue. Belief gives you what it takes to become a world-renowned innovator who makes history. Belief inspires you to be a game-changer, in areas where you once would have never had an opportunity to achieve victory.

The next time you are near a mirror, I want you to step directly in front of it. Pause for a moment and look directly at yourself. Declare the following words, as you accept the belief of your excellence: *I am a masterpiece of my Heavenly Father! Victory is in my DNA! Triumph is flowing through my veins! No challenge will hold me down! I have what it takes to succeed! I will achieve success!*

How do you feel now that you have said those words? How do you feel now that you are speaking your excellence into existence? Do you believe these declarations of your beliefs more, now that you have said them aloud? Has positively telling yourself who you are, and what you have, made an impact of any kind on you? Are you gaining a belief that greater days are ahead of you in your future?

Speaking greatness into existence upon your life is one of the best ways to increase the status of positive beliefs in your life. It opens windows to blessings that pour out in your life. In spite of this, it still takes the will on your part to make it happen. What you bring to the situation is what you get from the situation.

For the next seven days, I want you to take sixty full, uninterrupted seconds to stand in front of a mirror and look directly at yourself. As you see the beauty of yourself that God has made in His image, I want you to boldly declare these words: *I believe I will achieve my victory! I believe God will show His power in my life! I believe I am blessed!* For sixty full, uninterrupted seconds each day, continually repeat the words of these declarations. Meditate for the complete, continuous time of the full minute upon the greatness that God has placed within you, through the use of these words. Allow victory to reside in your beliefs, as you optimistically speak your beliefs into existence.

Victory will come to you, if you believe it will come to you. When you believe victory will come to you, you take the necessary actions to make it come to you. Belief stretches you from small points of performance to great prosperity in areas unanticipated by man. Belief brings about the victory of goals that were once regarded to you as elusive. Belief allows your faith to overpower the negative voices in your mind that do their best to tear down your spirit of victory. Through this, a faithful spirit is stirred up within you that makes you fight and overcome your challenges.

My friend, to have the faithful, fighting spirit within you that is needed to achieve victory, backing away from victory cannot be what you do in the face of challenges. Many times, we think that backing up into some part of the past will fix our situation, but this tends to be one of the worst things that we can do when faced with adversity. Even if you spend mere seconds backing yourself up into the past each day during your times of difficulty, these seconds have the power to bring about very harmful outcomes in our lives.

Think of the last time you were in a parking space, and you got in your car with the intent to leave. What did you do? You began to back up. Just as backing up in a car takes only a few seconds, the same may ring true about dwelling on the past for a small amount of time each day. Nevertheless, in the small amount of time that a driver backs up, a high number of accidents occur. On the same note, dwelling upon your past at small points during the day may bring about spiritual accidents of all kinds that will impede your victory.

To move forward to victory, your mind cannot hinder you to live in the past. A victor does not move forward in life, with the possession of a pessimistic outlook on the present. Having a negative state of mind overshadows hope for a better tomorrow. Keep in mind that hope is a central part of the very definition of what faith happens to be. "Now faith is the substance of things hoped for, the evidence of things not seen" (Hebrews 11:1 KJV).

Hope is the anticipation of God's favor being expressed in life, which is why it is such a vital part of what faith is defined to be. God is not just *"a"* hope for realizing your dreams. He is *"the"* hope! The article *"a"* in the English language is an indefinite article, but there is nothing indefinite about the power of God. On the other hand, *"the"* is a definite article in the English language, and the power of God is the definite hope, upon which your beliefs should reside. While the difference between these two articles is often overlooked, it is frequently *"a"* difference that means *"the"* difference between victory and defeat, many times in life.

Just as God is the basis for our definite hope for victory, He is also our definite Master and Savior. God deserves definite praise at all times! "The LORD is my strength and my defense; He has become my salvation. He is my God, and I will praise Him" (Exodus 15:2 NIV). Regardless of what you are facing, give God praise! Giving praise to God shows Him that you believe your blessings will come to you. Praising Him instills the faith within your spirit that is needed to fight to achieve victory. Showing praise to the Lord builds confidence within you, as it strengthens your beliefs.

How do you praise God? Pause for a moment with me. I want you to decide how you will show praise to God. If you can sing, I want you to express your praise to Him with songs. If you are a poet, I want you to express your praise to Him with poetry. If you are a public speaker, I want you to express your praise to Him through speech. If you are a teacher, I want you to express your praise to Him through teaching others about God's greatness. If your praise is in the form of a dance, praise the Lord with the most excellent movements that flow through your spirit.

Despite your differences from others in the manner that you show praise to God, I want you to make it a daily routine to show God praise! Pause with me for a moment to connect with the Lord. Let this be the first time, in the regular routine, in which you begin to show our Savior praise with the gift that He has blessed you with to show Him praise. In whatever fashion that you most like to use to uplift the name of the Lord, do it here, as you read with me. From singing to writing, however you give God praise, pause for a moment and do it. Regardless of how you do it, or how long you need in order to pause and exalt our Master, please pause and do it!

How do you feel now that you have magnified the name of the Lord in the manner that you best see fit? Has it connected you more to Him? Do you feel closer to Him at this very moment? As you uplift the name of our Father, always keep in mind that you must do so in the way that you best see fit. Magnifying the name of God uplifts Him to you, and it makes you closer to Him. It makes your connection to Him stronger, and it makes your worries about the problems you face weaker.

My friend, I cannot encourage you enough to give praise to God. Praise the Lord, when the sun shines in your life. Praise the Lord, during the midnight hour. Praise the Lord, knowing that He and He alone has all power!

By using praise as your weapon, you are able to move forward to the mountaintop of victory. As praise lives within you and shines through you, blessings will rain down upon you, stronger than any droplet of doubt or discouragement ever could. With praise as your weapon against any challenge that may present itself before you,

you are bringing forth the favor of God to shine upon you. In essence, you are opening the door to your blessings through praise, regardless how far or impossible your blessings may seem for you to reach. Through your praise to our Father, you are able to see the impossible become reality. As you praise God, you are showing others that there is nothing that you believe He cannot do in your life, and you also believe there is nothing that He cannot bless you to do.

> **"Those who say it can't be done are usually interrupted by those doing it."**
> **—James A. Baldwin**

Let your praise to the Lord reign over any rain of troublesome times that may fall upon you. Instead of worrying, give God praise. Instead of doubting, give God praise. Instead of complaining, give God praise.

Every moment of your praise gives thanks to God. As we praise God, we show our thankfulness to Him in His glory. When we thank God before we even receive our victory, we are releasing faith over our challenges. Let words like these flow from your lips, in spite of what is taking place in your life: *Lord, thank You for bringing me out of this. Heavenly Father, thank You for the blessings You have in store for me. God, thank You for my victory.* By thanking God before you receive your blessings, you are allowing your actions to demonstrate your belief that you will be blessed.

Let your actions of praise show your thankfulness to our Heavenly Father. Thank Him for the lessons that you will learn from your obstacles. Thank Him for the greatness that He has in store for you. Thank Him for the doors of the past that He has closed. Thank Him for the triumphs ahead of you that He is bringing to you by closing those doors. Thank Him for the doors of today that He has opened. Thank Him for the doors of tomorrow that He will open. As you thank the Lord, you allow your faith to take a strong stand against any challenge that may present itself before you.

We often do not realize that the praise we give to God serves as one of the most vital spiritual weapons of success. The thanks that we give to God is one of the strongest forms of praise; it serves as a key ingredient of our unconditional praise to the Lord! Notice that giving thanks is an *action*, not simply a *thought*. This goes to show that it takes effort on your part to give thanks to the Lord, and this allows you to see the greatness in even the worst situations.

Close your eyes. Think of one challenge in your life that you have been striving to overcome, yet it still lives in your life. What comes to mind for you when you think of this challenge? Is it something that you want to stand your ground against? Do you want to become the victor against the challenge, not the victim? Give God praise and uplift His name each time that you begin to doubt the outcome of your challenge. At points, when uncertainty comes to mind as to how your situation will turn out, magnify the Lord so that you will lessen the power of your problems. In cohesion with kneeling to God in prayer, lift your head to Him in praise.

Praise brings silence to the rage of the thunders of trouble. When praise to the Lord comes through you, a smile is the expression that comes to your face, no matter how discouraging the present moment may seem to others. When praise to the Lord comes through you, gladness exists within your heart in all situations. When praise to the Lord comes through you, you are able to clearly connect with Him.

Allow the eyes of your faith to be what you use to view the good and bad in your life. Let faith be the lens you look through to see life's happenings. By doing this, you look beyond the natural and you see that God has blessings waiting for you in the supernatural, despite how things may seem at this moment. While the natural eyes may see nothing taking place on your behalf in your life, the eyes of faith see great things taking place behind the scenes on your behalf. When you see greatness awaiting you, this inspires you to deliver a powerful form of praise to the Lord.

Praise brings calmness within your spirit. Giving praise to the Lord puts you on one accord with Him. Praise is a powerful factor that prepares you for victory. My friend, praise generates blessings to flow upon you as the hand of God releases them to you. Instead of having doubt, give praise to God. Instead of worrying, give praise to God. Instead of being in a lane of life when you think it is best to complain, give praise to God. Complaints get you nowhere, but praise takes you anywhere.

Demonstrating praise to God through your actions illustrates the faith within your spirit. To be blessed, you must first have the faith that your blessings will come. Through your praise to our Heavenly Father, you are preparing the place before you to receive your blessings. When you praise God, you expect greatness to be displayed in your life. Praising God shows your faith in action. Through praising God, you give a solid foundation to your beliefs. After your beliefs have a solid foundation, victory has a place to reside in your life.

When it comes to praise, I can picture a woman who sang a well-known gospel song about God's greatness, in front of a massive crowd of people. She did this shortly before going to the hospital for surgery. In the eyes of many other individuals, there is no way that they would even consider doing this. A woman in the audience was even so bold as to express the words, "Why would you sing in front of other people right before surgery? She's crazy! I would never do what she is doing!"

Knowing that many people were probably thinking what this woman in the audience was whispering to the person next to her, the singer felt the need to pause and give God even more praise. She stated before the audience, "While there are many people who probably would not stand here doing what I am doing, if they were in my shoes, this is what God has inspired me to do. I am giving Him the praise He deserves, because I know it will touch the right person's heart in the right way." This woman was wearing the shoes that God prepared for her, not the shoes of anyone else. As such, she was able to do what He called her to do, at the time He called her to do it. The encouraging woman was able to give God praise in the manner that He spoke to her to show her praise.

Months later, this same woman was able to stand before another crowd to speak of God's greatness, just before she sang once again. Not only was she blessed to make it through the surgery, but she now had a testimony as to what praise can do! She had a testimony as to how victory will come to you, when you believe in the power of God to move in your life!

I was very motivated by the way this woman was allowing her belief in the excellence of God to be expressed. Her belief stood behind her faith, and her faith led her to the victory of making it through surgery. No matter what the "surgery" that you are approaching in your life happens to be, still give God praise! See the "surgery" as a challenge that God is using to make you better. Keep your faith strong within your spirit. Let your praise ring out, as you continually honor God. Praise brings forth expectance. When you praise God, you expect greatness to be displayed in your life. Through praising God, you give a solid foundation to your beliefs. When your beliefs have a solid foundation, victory has a place to reside in your life.

Chapter Four

THE HEARTBEAT OF TRIUMPH

Pause with me for a moment. Take your hand and place it on your chest. Feel the beat of your heart as it touches your hand. What does it feel like? How does the beat of your heart continue to go on and on, despite what is happening now, what happened five minutes ago, or what will happen five minutes from now? It is because your heart is not a passive part of you; it is active. Your heart actively keeps you alive, and it keeps your body working as a whole. The beat of your heart is the center of the very reason why you are alive. Just as this is true, the heartbeat of your dreams is the very core of triumph coming into your life.

Triumph is not the result of passively awaiting what *may* happen. It is the product of actively anticipating what *will* happen. What we *expect* to happen raises the bar for what *will* happen. When we anticipate greatness, great things happen. On the same token, when we anticipate failures, we succumb to those failures.

> "Many of life's failures are people who did not realize how close they were to success when they gave up."
>
> —Thomas A. Edison

Your expectations are your approaches to your blessings. My friend, your expectations represent what you believe. Your hopes represent what you believe. Your anticipations represent what you believe. Let your hopeful anticipation meet your confident expectation, as it stirs up your self-assured motivation.

Our expectations are *always* in action. Because our expectations are always in action, one other thing is always in action: *faith*. There is never a day or time when faith is passive. Faith is an active part of you that is always working. It never takes a day off, and it never stops moving. With that being the case, questions like these tend to flood your mind: *If faith is so strong, then why do I lose so many times? If faith is so strong, then why am I still where I have asked God to bless me to rise above? If faith is so strong, why do I want to be right, but I am always wrong?* All of these questions can be answered by the *lane* where your faith is traveling.

There are two lanes in which your faith can travel, and two directions in which those lanes guide your faith. When you expect victory to be the outcome of your battle, your faith travels in the lane with a destination of triumph. However, when you expect defeat to be the outcome of your battle, your faith travels in the lane with a destination of disappointment.

When you sit down to take a test with the thought, "I'm going to fail this test," your faith is leading you to failure. When you walk into a courtroom with the thought, "I'm going to lose this case," your faith is leading you to failure. When you walk into an interview with the thought, "I'll never get a job like this," your faith is leading you to failure. As long as your beliefs lead you in one direction, that is the direction where you will travel.

In contrast to disappointments coming from embracing negative beliefs as the foundation of your expectations, triumph comes from embracing positive beliefs as the foundation of your expectations. As an optimistic student who sits down to take a test with the confident thought, "I'm going to do well on this test," your faith is leading you to triumph! By walking into a courtroom with the thought, "I will win this case," your faith is leading you to triumph! As you enter a conference room for an interview with the thought, "I will get this job," your faith is leading you to triumph! When your faith leads you in the direction of triumph, this is what beats within your heart in the midst of any challenge.

> "You can be pitiful, or you can be powerful, but you can't be both."
>
> —Joyce Meyer

Let me guide you to make a stronger connection to what I am saying. I want you to make a connection between what is now happening in your life, and what you expect to be the outcome of it. Close your eyes for a moment. As you do so, think of five things that are taking place in your life. It does not matter how major or minor they are, just picture those things in your mind. How do you think they will turn out? What do you expect to be the outcome?

As you did this with me, were your answers to my questions from a positive frame of mind, or a negative one? Were you optimistic about the outcome, or pessimistic? My friend, I cannot say enough about how much we tend to live out what we believe will happen. With small things, it is so much easier to be optimistic about what we believe will happen. Nevertheless, with big things, it is much easier to be pessimistic about what we believe will happen. Despite wanting to be blessed, there are still many people who embrace the mindset of disappointment. Before even putting forth a slight amount of effort, so many individuals already expect to lose. When you expect negative things, you will receive negative things. On the other hand, when you expect great things, you will receive great things. In order to have victory, we must first believe that victory will be the end result of what is taking place in our lives.

Instead of hanging your head in defeat, kneel to God in prayer. Desperate times call for faith-filled prayers! Through prayer, you illuminate faith. With faith, you will prompt the hand of God to move in your favor. When faith resides within your spirit, triumph is able to beat within your heart. Triumph beats within your heart because God brings victory to you, as a result of your belief in His power. Just as you dance to the beat of a song that plays in the background, the same rings true with the beat of your heart.

Don't let your heart beat to the rhythm of your problems. Allow God to cleanse your heart, as you embrace His purifying hand. "Create in me a clean heart, O God; and renew a right spirit within me" (Psalm 51:10 KJV). Pray to the Lord for Him to create a clean heart within you, so that triumph will beat strongly within your spirit. Let the triumphant beats of your heart pattern themselves on the same wavelength with an optimistic state of your mind.

No matter what challenge you are looking to overcome, triumph will never beat in your heart when doubt controls your state of mind. Doubt cannot live within you when faith moves through you. Faith multiplies your blessings, and subtracts from your worries. Don't give life to doubt, but give birth to faith through positive beliefs.

Faith is the fuel of God's work in our lives. To see His work happen in our favor, we must have faith. Our expectations are in line with our faith. The expectations we have serve as self-fulling prophesies in our lives. To have change, we must expect change.

It is so easy to physically change something when it is associated with our leisure. If we dislike the song on the radio, we change the radio to another station. If we dislike the show on television, we change the television to another channel. However, what about when something is taking place in life that is not as easy as pressing a button to bring about change? A change may seem hard to make, but there is one place you should focus to make that change: *your mind.*

Your mind is clearly the key to empowering faith within you. When your mental expectations rest upon the favor of God bringing blessings into your life, faith will rest within your spirit. With faith as the foundation of the expectations of our blessings, we see God's work in action. When we expect the favor of the Lord, we receive His favor. By expecting to be blessed, we *will* be blessed.

In order for you to expect positive things to happen, you must see the positive before it happens. For each moment that you see the negative, you will be overcome by the negative. With every second that you expect setbacks, you will not step forward. Worldly patterns make us merely see the situations of life from the natural view. However, heavenly patterns make us see the situations of life from a faith-filled view. By having a faith-filled view of life, we are able to change our mindset from thoughts of doubt to a highly assured level of confidence. "Do not conform to the pattern of this world, but be transformed by the renewing of your mind" (Romans 12:2 NIV).

When faith becomes friends with adversity, we are able to use the challenges that come before us as stepping stones toward triumph. Adversity teaches us how to seize the day of our dreams, and how to have faith that makes us never let them go. In times like these, faith prompts us not to succumb to flippant views of life in the face of obstacles, but to hold strong to our visions of victory. Viewing the positive over the negative inspires our state of mind to allow us to shine.

Pessimism does its best to hold you back from the optimistic state of mind needed for you to move forward. Doubt works avidly to steer you in the opposite direction of victory, and make defeat your perfect shoe size. At the very time that I am writing this book, the news is inundated in the background with negative reports. Developing stories of people dying because of accidents in the midst of flooding have been some of the most reported stories in the past couple of days. This has heightened, even in the last few hours.

While it is good to know what may take place around us, only seeing life's negative happenings conditions our minds to expect negativity. When we expect negative things to happen, we limit ourselves to let downs. By expecting negative happenings, we close our eyes to our blessings. My friend, you cannot embrace success until you close your eyes to the negative and open them to the positive. Once your eyes open to the positive, faith moves your footsteps. When you step out on faith, you step over doubt.

> "Take the first step in faith. You don't have to see the whole staircase, just take the first step."
> –Martin Luther King, Jr.

Faith lets the light shine before you so that you are able to take footsteps into success. There are so many times in life when we adopt the mode of thinking that the challenges we face are what will hold us back from our blessings. Do not believe this for one second. The challenge is not the problem. Not being prepared for the challenge is the problem. Faith prepares you for any challenge, and the hand of God blesses you to conquer the challenge.

You cannot simply allow your mind to automatically press the "negative" button when a challenge presents itself to you. Remove negativity from being the autopilot of your life, and get in the driver's seat yourself with high expectations of being blessed. Don't automatically embrace negativity, but naturally embrace optimism. No matter how difficult the obstacles you are facing may appear, still keep the faith. The bright times of a new day are headed your way. Always remember that God turns a time of mourning into the brightness of a new morning, when faith lives within you.

Too often, we think that we need a large happening to move us to a greater place in life. My friend, please know that is not the case. Consider the fact that to move greatness into your life, all you need is faith the size of a mustard seed. Many people believe that a mustard seed is too small to make anything happen. Even so, a mustard seed is smaller than a physical key that opens a physical door. Just by looking at the size of a physical key and the size of a physical door, how could something so small open something so much bigger? It is because it was made to happen that way. In the same way, faith was made to work in combination with the hand of God to bless you. A mustard seed is what God put into place to open the doors of your opportunities.

Just think of the simple thing that God is asking from you for you to be blessed. He wants you to have a small size of faith, as you believe that you will receive your blessings. In the game of life, it is up to us to follow the plays that God calls from His playbook. By doing this, we will result in receiving positive yardage on the path to pursuing our goals. Regardless of what problem presents itself in front of you, let faith be your fight song!

As you follow the plays in the game of life, don't concede to defeat. My friend, for every setback you face, God has already prepared a setup for a triumphant comeback. You must have the ability to move beyond one bad play in the game of life, and empower yourself to move forward. No matter how badly one situation may seem, you can't dwell on it in order to be successful. Don't hold the old. Break through to the new. Don't cry over stumbles of the past. Celebrate the blessings ahead of you, before they even happen!

Don't simply hang your head with acceptance of the belief that you will not be a victor of your circumstances. You cannot accept the view that you will be a victim of a challenge. Hold your head up high, and embrace the belief that you will be blessed. Blessings do not have a slow season. Opportunity never takes a day off from its right time of knocking. Although *opportunity* may appear to be just another word in the dictionary, its impact is as big as the Atlantic Ocean.

Despite how things may appear today, keep the faith that the right opportunity for you is on the way! No matter how good or bad a situation may seem, opportunities will still present themselves to you. You can't control the circumstances, but you can control your approach to those circumstances. When you approach life's circumstances with faith and expectancy, triumph awaits you. Approaching a circumstance with a faith-filled spirit allows triumph to beat in your heart.

My friend, faith will quench your thirst for triumph, regardless what obstacles stand before you. No matter how big the obstacles before you may appear, always let this knowledge reverberate in your mind. Despite the problems that may present themselves before you, faith keeps the hand of God upon you.

> **"The will of God will never take you to where the grace of God will not protect you."**
> —Bernadette Devlin

God knows when you'll need Him, where you'll need Him, and why you'll need Him, in every set of circumstances in your life.

There are so many times that bad things happening today tend to steer our minds away from the great things God has done for us in the past. In order to be blessed, we must remember what God has already done in our lives. As we remember what God has already done for us, we are able to expect Him to do great things in our lives in the future. How do you expect to have triumph over the challenges you are facing, when you are allowing your previous triumphs to now be simple, everyday happenings?

Take a moment to connect with one big thing that God has done in your past. Look up to the sky for a moment. Clear your mind. Now, allow thoughts of the big happening that took place in your past to be all that controls your mind for the next sixty seconds. Let your mind be filled with images of what took place during that time. Just as the hand of God moved at that time in your life, it will move again in your favor. All you need is faith that God will bless you, in order to receive your blessings. Faith brings about the hand of God, at just the right moment, in your favor.

Instead of viewing your challenges as ending points of your life, see them as stepping stones to the victories that await you. My friend, God tends to show you the same thing from a different point of view, and He uses that different point of view to make you a better you. With the different point of view that our Heavenly Father gives you to make you a better you, He empowers you to stand strong against the challenges you face. You can use the eyes of failure or you can use the eyes of faith to view your challenges. Even though you may be looking at the same thing, the *way* you look at it is ultimately what counts.

The challenges you overcome today empower you to overcome even greater challenges tomorrow, so that you will achieve greater victories. Your victories over your challenges make you a living testimony to the power of God in action. Despite what may be taking place in your life, just remember how the hand of God has already moved in your life on your behalf.

No year ever passes without you making at least one accomplishment. I'll show you what I mean. Think of five accomplishments that you have made in the last five years, one for each year. Write each of these down. Place your hand on what you have written. Now, close your eyes and meditate upon why these are accomplishments, not failures. For the next seven days, I want you to add one accomplishment to these five, before you go to bed. After doing so, I want you to pause for at least two minutes, and meditate upon why these are accomplishments and not failures. Repeat this process each day of the next seven days.

Do not only use meditation as a cleansing of the mind, but also as a way to connect with the Word of God. For the next four weeks, select a weekly scripture upon which to meditate. Learn the scripture. Recite the scripture. Cleanse your mind with the words of the scripture. Gain an understanding of the scripture. During positive points of your days, reflect upon the words of the scripture. During negative points of your days, reflect upon words of the scripture.

I cannot say enough about how much meditation levels the playing field in life. Meditation is time spent searching the soul. This is a practice that blesses you to close your natural eyes to daily dilemmas, as you open the eyes of faith to see a vision of excellence. "Where there is no vision, the people perish" (Proverbs 29:18 KJV). Closing your eyes to problems lets you open your eyes to greatness.

As we meditate, we gain vision through our faith. When we meditate, God's hand calms our spirit, as He allows us to see that He has and will continue to bless our lives. By having the eyes of your faith open to see the hand of God in action, there is no work of our Father that is too massive for you to see Him overcome, despite how it may appear to the natural eye. Closing your eyes to problems lets you open your eyes to excellence. Always take the time to let the calming effects of meditation soothe your life. My friend, do not rob yourself of the benefits that taking the time to relax and recall God's excellence has. Meditation prepares us to see the Lord's greatness in action by reminding us of His glorious power.

Too often, we become forgetful of what God has done in our lives, when obstacles present themselves before us. It may seem as if the more you strive to overcome a challenge, the more the challenge appears to overcome you. If this is the way you see your challenge, you must adjust your view. In order to conquer the challenge, the way you look at the challenge has to change. Don't merely look at your challenge as something designed to hold you back. See it as a point used to move you forward. In order to move forward and not be held back, you must find the positive in even the most negative of situations. As long as you still view your challenges from the same defeated angle that you previously had, victory is not in your path. Triumph does not beat in the midst of negativity. The triumphant heart does not beat with a repackaged, doubtful forecast.

Surround yourself with positive features. Inundate yourself with positive people. Flood your thoughts with positive views of the seemingly bad things that are taking place now in your life. Let optimism illuminate through the eyes of your faith, as you view life from a hopeful standpoint. While doing this, many things happen to your health. Instead of sneezing with suspicion, you are being healed with hope. Instead of your heart skipping beats with doubt, it beats stronger awaiting triumph.

Have you ever paused to realize that not only does your spiritual health improve by having faith, but your physical health also does? Think of being at a job where it appears that the harder you work, the worse things seem to become. One big health issue may happen as a result of this: *high blood pressure.* Headaches and many other physical health problems may come from this one health problem. Not only that, mental health problems may span from these things, as well.

It may seem as if the problems that surround you on the job come with you, no matter where you go. Has someone ever asked you how your day was, and this led you to embrace a spirit of negativity? You just wanted to flood their ears with the problematic situations that have not only taken place that week, not even just that day, but just in the last hour that you were on the job? All of this is because of one word: *problem.* When you allow a problem to control your thoughts, you allow negativity to control your thoughts. The more negativity controls your thoughts, the further you move away from faith.

Whether on the job, or at any point in everyday life, problems tend to span from giving others control of our lives. We have problems when we give others control of who we are. How much do the words of others affect your beliefs? How much does another person's opinion of you affect who you are? For every second that you think about the negative opinions that others have of you, you are giving them power over you. At any point when you allow another person's negative views against you to control your thoughts, you are giving that person power over you. By allowing another person to control your mind, you are giving that person power over you.

> "The greatest prison people live in is the fear of what other people think."
>
> — David Icke

Don't let your focus rest upon satisfying your critics. If a person's true intent was to help you, then that person's focus would not rest upon finding your faults. Concentrate on making yourself better, based on how you see yourself being better, not based on how others see you being better.

For every second that you spend worrying whether or not others like you, you are wasting precious points of your life. These are moments that could be spent raising the bar of who you are. With every moment that you spend wondering what you can do to look better in the eyes of your critics, you are wasting valuable moments that could be better spent removing limits from yourself. My friend, don't concentrate on the need to receive awards from man when God has much greater things in store for you.

> "Man gives you the award, but God gives you the reward."
> —Denzel Washington

What another person *thinks* of you is a *little* thing. What you *know* about yourself is a *big* thing. Clear your mind with me for a moment. Ask yourself this question: *Who am I?* Now, allow as many things to rush to your mind as possible that speak to how you can answer this question. Once you have done this, pick three things that you feel best speak to who you are, and say them aloud. After doing this, you have spoken to who you are. You have taken power over yourself to speak your own greatness into existence. By answering that question, yourself, you took ownership of your own identity.

Too often, our critics tend to come about, because they don't feel that we are walking in the "right footsteps." Instead of stepping out in our own shoes, our critics often like for us to limit ourselves to where they *think* we should be, not where we *know* we should be. Don't concentrate on following in the footsteps of another person. Focus on moving beyond those footsteps.

Your faith is what moves you into a blessing. Faith doesn't just walk to the door of a blessing. It makes an entrance into it. When you keep the faith, your focus rests upon the person you *know* you are, not who others want you to be. Focus on knowing who you are, and not allowing anyone else to take that from you.

When you know who you are, and you take ownership of who you are, you stop others from defining your identity. Another person's opinion of you never gains the power to materialize until you give it power. The opinions that others have of you are *little* things. Those opinions are not facts. My friend, don't focus your attention upon the little things in life. Don't lose great opportunities because of your focus resting upon the little things in life. Let your focus rest upon faith.

Opportunities tend to pass us by when we don't look at our circumstances through the eyes of faith. Your current circumstances may seem to be the worst in the world, from one glance; however, a glance with faith could change your whole perspective. Even at times when God has the best opportunities presented to us, we may look beyond them because we feel that we are not where we should be. Never think that you are in the "wrong place" at the "wrong time." Keep in mind that God's time is *always* the *right* time.

Our Heavenly Father always has a purpose behind where He has placed you. The very place where you are, is where God put you. It is no coincidence. If you were meant to be anywhere else at this very second, God would have you there. You are reading this very page of this very book, at this very moment, for a reason. It's God's work in action. God knows when to put you in a place, where to place you, how to place you, and why to place you there.

For success to be the outcome of the goals you pursue, keeping faith within you as you trust in God is what is required of you. Success is everything you make of it; not what others make of you. By drawing a close connection between yourself and the Lord, you steer yourself toward success. While there is a 99.99% chance with man, there is a 100% chance with God!

To have success, you must pursue success. Even if it appears that the gifts that God has given you to be successful are of no use, don't embrace that belief. Regardless if it seems that the skills that God gave you are not true blessings, don't think that way.

Questions such as these tend to come to mind when times get hard: *If this is such a skill, then why is it of no use? If this is such a blessing, then why are no doors being opened with it? If this is such a gift, then why am I not moving forward with it?* My friend, never allow this type of thinking to lead your state of mind. The moment that this appears to happen, look to the Lord for guidance. What He may be working to show you is that the skills He has given you are being *developed*. He may be showing you that the blessings that you already have are leading into even larger blessings.

Don't wallow in worries of when the ultimate triumph over your challenges will come. Be thankful for the triumphs that you have today. Celebrate the triumphs you achieve today. No matter how big or small, praise God for your triumphs. The triumphs that you have today may not be as big as those that will come tomorrow, but they are placing you on the path to achieve them. God orders your steps with small victories so that you will be blessed with large victories, when the time is right.

When the time is right, the right doors will open in your favor. If the door was opened on your timing, not God's timing, it could close before your greatness would ever be shown. The same door, opening when God knows the time is right, may open and have an immeasurable number of blessings flowing out of it. This is why we are on God's time, not our time. Just because our time is not God's time does not mean that He will not bring success into our lives. To be blessed, you cannot have an inability to delay gratification. You must be able to move when and where the hand of God guides you.

There are times in life when you may feel that you have been striving to reach a goal, but you have made no progress. Keep in mind that God puts things on hold when you aren't ready. The season in which the Lord has currently placed you may be the season that will bring about your needed growth. Your current season of life may be one that appears to be holding you back from your blessings. It may present itself as a time of one challenge after another. Even so, never think of a challenge as something that will stop you.

Challenges make you mature in your faith. Challenges make your faith flourish. The eyes of faith are what you use to face your challenges. There are times when challenges may blind us to viewing the blessings ahead of us. Even so, there is no challenge that faith cannot overcome. Spiritual blindness is healed through the eyes of faith. When you face your challenges head on with faith, you are able to conquer them.

"It's lack of faith that makes people afraid of meeting challenges."

—Muhammad Ali

One of the biggest challenges that we face in life is timing. Timing is one of the biggest problems we have with the receipt of our blessings. The timing we desire for the receipt of our blessings often lacks cohesion with the receipt of our blessings. God's time is always the *set* time, regardless of when our aspiration for the best time happens to be. If you are not receiving your blessings on your timetable, just remind yourself of this: *God has a reason for every season*. Even if it appears that you have done everything that you can possibly do to be blessed, yet you still have not reached your goal, don't spend your time trying to figure out our Heavenly Father's plan. He knows what He is doing, when He is doing it, where He is doing it, how He is doing it, and why He is doing it. God does not need our help with His timetable.

The more we attempt to figure out God's plans, the more we tend to confuse ourselves. If we can't figure out the small things in life, how do we expect to figure out the plans of our Heavenly Master? Don't spend your time trying to decide whether or not keeping the faith in troubled times makes sense. Rest assured, knowing that having faith is what will lead you to an overflow of blessings.

"Faith doesn't make sense. It makes miracles."
— Dr. Tony Evans

Don't spend your time counting down the days of your life, in a rush to meet your goal. If you have not yet received your blessing, it is not time for you to receive it. Spend your time advancing yourself forward in life. Focus on what you can do to make yourself a better you. My friend, you only have one life to live, so live it to your best!

"Don't count the days. Make the days count."
— Muhammad Ali

Our arrival at the destination of our blessings will come in due time, and God knows when, where, and why that time happens to be. With this in mind, we should not waste our time trying to rush any moment of time. Instead of merely concentrating on the destination of your blessings, step back and take a look at what's happening during your journey. To appreciate a destination, you must first appreciate the journey. God's timetable may be occurring the way that it is in order to show us something in life.

Many times, I have heard others make comments like, "God's not doing anything for me," or, "The more I pray, the more I hear silence!" Silence speaks volumes, but we must have faith in order to be able to listen to what God is saying through the silence. Is His pause through silence simply a test of faith? Is the pause a tool that God is using to reinvigorate your passion? Despite the purpose of the pause before your blessings, keep in mind that God's timetable is always the right timetable.

Even during my time writing this book, I have seen God's timetable in action, and how far it surpasses mine. There have been so many days when it was in my plan to work on this book, but it wasn't in God's plan. My time was shifted by so many circumstances that I often didn't have the opportunity to continue my work for months. Nevertheless, when it was in God's plan for me to continue, I could effortlessly continue from the exact spot where I stopped, with no inhibitions. Not only that, the pauses in my time of writing provided me with even more inspirational words to convey. I simply allow points in my life like these to demonstrate to me that God's time is *always* the best time, even when it is not my time.

Not only does our timing often differ with God's timing, our plans also often tend to differ. Although God's plan is not always our plan, it is always a much better plan. You may only think the sum of 8+6 is coming to you, and you may be angered when you don't receive this on your time schedule. However, God may, instead, be sending the product of 8x6 to you, which is a much bigger value than you expected. This is a key example that God not only blesses us when we follow Him, but He blesses us with much more than we would have imagined.

"And let us not be weary in well doing: for in due season we shall reap, if we faint not" (Galatians 6:9 KJV). The right doors will open for you at the right times, and the right people will be standing behind them. Not only are you pregnant with possibility, you will give birth to the reality of your blessings when you have faith. With faith, your cup won't run dry. Your cup will run over with blessings.

A significant problem that people often have when it comes to waiting on the receipt of blessings happens to be feeling embarrassed by the opinions of others. When it appears that a goal may not be reached, due to the long period of time that it is taking to be blessed with it, our faith tends to waver. We often adhere to the natural instinct of becoming embarrassed by what others think of us, in terms of how we appear when we have not achieved our goals. My friend, don't let timing cause you to lose faith in yourself, or in the power of God. Faith turns an embarrassment into an empowerment.

Let your certainty overpower your uncertainty. Allow your prayers to rest upon the foundation of your faith. You cannot have selective beliefs regarding what will take place as a result of your prayers. One prayer cannot have faith as its essence, while the other has doubt as its essence. Blessings will not be the outcome of both if this is the case. Faith brings serenity. Doubt brings worry. The more time spent having faith, the closer you come to being blessed. On the other hand, the more time spent being worried, the further you move away from your blessings.

Despite how things may appear today, don't give up on God's power to bless you. My friend, you cannot control each moment of your life, but you can control your responses to the moments of your life. Each response we make is a choice. Choices don't simply affect you today, but also for days throughout generations to come. There are many times when we simply want to prepare our responses to happenings in life before they even take place, especially in times of adversity. One problem often exists with this. We tend to allow negative responses to be what we have prepared for how we will respond to our obstacles. Why is that? It is because of the words that we allow our minds to use to paint our thoughts, regarding the happenings in our lives.

Words have tremendous power. One word can change the whole atmosphere. Words provide invitations into our lives, both good and bad. Words can motivate you to fight on until the end, or discourage you to lie down in defeat, when you are so close to victory.

> "You may encounter many defeats, but you must never be defeated."
>
> — Maya Angelou

Think of the last time someone's words were so strong that they caused your heart to race unexpectedly. Let these be words of kindness that caught you off guard so much that you would not have anticipated hearing them. Now, I want you to do the same task, but let's change it a bit. Reflect upon the last time someone's hostile, aggressive words caused your heart to race unexpectedly. What was similar about the two situations? What was different about the two situations? There was one thing that caused a significant difference between the two situations: *words*.

Another person's words may have an effect on you, but *your* words have the strongest influence over you. Your words can solidify your victory, or they can talk you out of victory. Your words can close your eyes to defeat, as they open your eyes to victory. My friend, the words that we speak over ourselves are more powerful to talk ourselves out of victory, or into victory, than those that any another person may speak.

Let the words you speak be a trail to triumph, not a trap that holds you back from it. The obstacles you face may come against you from an unstoppable standpoint in the eyes of man. Even so, speak these words to your obstacles: *I come victoriously against you in the name of Jesus! Move aside as I claim my place on the mountaintop of my triumph!*

Let your words speak faith into existence, despite the type of situation you happen to be enduring. As you speak words of faith, you are able to see life through the eyes of faith. To be blessed, you must first have the faith that your blessings will come. Prophesying your blessings is a successful fashion used to bring them forth. Regardless how big or small the challenge in your life happens to be, speak a prophecy in your favor. Speak a prophecy of triumph over adversity. Speak a prophecy of victory over defeat. Speak a prophecy of faith over failure. Speak greatness over your life. Each moment you prophesy greatness for your life, you give even more substance to what you hope for, and you strengthen the foundation of what you do not see.

Despite what the challenge is that you are facing, only verbalize words of optimism about this obstacle. My friend, don't waste your words verbalizing negativity. Let positive words come from your mouth, or don't let any come at all. Don't give life to negativity by speaking it into existence. Only allow the seeds that your words plant in your life to be positive. Although negative thoughts may enter your mind at times, don't give those thoughts power by placing the breath of life behind them through verbalization. Realize that each breath you take is a gift from God, so don't let negativity impede your breath of life.

Embrace a mindset of optimism, and let an overflow of positively spoken words manifest from that mindset. I'm the type of person who is not afraid to speak his mind. Candor is a big part of who I am. This is highly disliked by some, yet admired by many others. My critics express words like, "He thinks he's so…" or "He's just too much for me!" Even during my time writing this book, the words of others have done their best to tear me down. In spite of this, I don't speak life into the words of my critics. I let negative words go in one ear and out of the other. Regardless what others have to say about you, still find the positive points about your situation and about yourself.

As you speak about what is happening with your challenge, and what will happen with it, remove words like these from your vocabulary: *impossible*, *defeat*, *incapable*, and *failure*. No matter what your challenge happens to be, embrace the belief that it is only a temporary part of your life, not permanent. Hold strong to the belief that the adversity you are facing is only a temporary setback. Accept the belief that even though you are facing a setback, it is actually a setup that will lead you to follow higher steps to a higher point in life. With positive beliefs like these that you are embracing, verbalize positive words that coincide with your positive beliefs, so that you will bring them to pass.

God shows us the power of prayer and words together as a result of our use of them together. Prayer is an important tool, but don't let your fight against your challenge stop with your prayers. Speak victory over your challenge. Speak triumph as the outcome of your situation. Speak excellence into existence, as you allow *victorious* to be the adjective that describes what is in you to stand up against any challenge.

By speaking victory over your life, you are releasing faith in the power of God against your obstacles. Each time even one thought of negativity toward yourself enters your mind, give the following words the power to flood your thoughts and defeat the negativity: *The Lord will bless me! Victory will be the outcome for me!* After you allow your mind to be flooded with such thoughts, verbalize them on a regular basis. Speak your blessings into existence. Let words of victory forecast greatness in your life.

Stand in front of the mirror. Look yourself directly in the eye. When you look in the mirror, say to yourself, "I see a winner! I see a victor! I see excellence!" Speak aloud the victory that you are working toward. Let your words highly set your mental standard for yourself. Don't simply speak to yourself saying, "I might be a conqueror." Boldly declare, "I am more than a conqueror!"

When you look at yourself in the mirror, let the eyes of faith be what you use to see yourself. The eyes of faith give you the view of a positive outlook. A positive outlook produces a positive outcome. With the eyes of faith opened to your blessings ahead, you are able to see the power of God in action.

At the same time, a negative outlook brings about a negative outcome. A negative outlook steers you toward negative words, and negative words give life to negative happenings. Complaints are some of the strongest examples of negativity taking its form. When you complain, it's like wearing a chain. Each complaint you make is like giving chains the power to pull you back, instead of having your positive prophecy move you forward. By loosening the chains that hold us back in life, the view of optimism becomes clear, with each situation we see.

The way we look at a set of circumstances does so much with how the situation is now, and how it will be in the future. Is there something happening in your life that is not to your liking? Step back and look at the situation. Are you a part of the problem? Is there something that you need to change to help the situation improve? Do you have a lack of faith that is causing a problem in your life? Don't just look outward to fix problems in your life. Begin by looking within.

Despite how a situation may look from one standpoint, remember there is always another way to look at it. You may be on the third floor of a situation, and it may only be in your plan to briefly go to the second floor. Even so, God may take you to the ground floor of that situation, as well as keep you there longer than you expected to be away from the third floor. Nevertheless, He may use your unexpected ground floor trip to be what you need to rise higher than your original third floor starting point.

Think about this for a moment: When was the last time you wanted to go to a point in life, but *you* were actually what held yourself back because of a fear of failure? Whether it was conscious or subconscious, why did you hold yourself back? Not pursuing a goal because you don't think you have what it takes lowers your limits. A lack of action on your part in these circumstances lowers the bar for you.

Pursuing a challenging goal gives you the peace of mind to know that you should put your best foot forward. Even if the realization of that goal does not happen at the time you want, having faith gives you the peace of mind to pursue the goal and realize the goal on God's timetable. When all appears to be against you, God will not only bless you to make an interception against adversity, but also a touchdown of triumph!

Too often, when I think of people who have held themselves back from goals that they were more than capable of achieving, the poem "Harlem" by the well-known poet Langston Hughes comes to mind. In the poem, he asks the following questions:

> **"What happens to a dream deferred? Does it dry up like a raisin in the sun? Or fester like a sore—And then run?"**
>
> **—Langston Hughes**

Close your eyes with me for a moment. As you do, reflect upon a goal that you once had, but you put off pursuing, because you felt there was something you lacked to achieve it. Let your feelings surrounding that situation come to mind next. My friend, let the emotions you presently feel, and those that you felt at that point in your life about that situation, come to mind. Are you glad you deferred the dream you once had? Do you think it is a good thing to hold yourself back because of self-doubt?

By deferring the steps that we need to take to reach a goal in life because of self-doubt, we place limits on ourselves. When a limitation is your expectation, this is exactly what you will receive: *a limitation*. However, when outcomes beyond limitations are your expectations, you will see the power of God in action in mighty ways. You will see God's works expressed in your favor.

Power of the natural hand is stopped due to limitations. Natural power paints the picture that your goals are impossible, and that they will never come to pass. However, God is supernatural. My friend, you don't serve a limited God. You serve an unlimited God with limitless power. By the grace of God, what appear to be errors written on one page of your life become excellence that turns you to a better page. Detours are often seen as the biggest errors that we come up against. Nevertheless, a detour is often what leads you to your proper destination. Always remember that God makes no errors. What are errors in the eyes of man are smoothing points on your path, through the eyes of faith.

You limit yourself from receiving blessings when you lack faith. This is because without faith, you forget that you serve a limitless God. Despite your circumstances, give glory to God! Thank God! Let the breath from your mouth express thanks to the Lord, by flooding through your words. As you do this while you await your blessings, you push aside your limitations. By doing this, you can see that you serve a limitless God. When you give thanks to God, your faith grows and the blessings that require this to come about flow upon you.

As your faith flourishes, you become closer to your goals in life. Have faith that your goals will come to pass. Declare that your goals will come to pass. Hope that your goals will come to pass. Believe that your goals will come to pass. Let each beat of your spiritual heart have an excessive overflow of hope, in spite of the obstacles that may present themselves before you.

Obstacles are not meant to overcome you. They are simply points in life meant to uplift you to greater heights in life, by bringing out the strength within you. It's not the obstacles that come, but how you overcome them that counts. Each obstacle that you face is merely a barrier for you to break down, so that you will advance to better places in life. Barriers must be broken for you to surpass what limits you.

The obstacles that challenge you in life are overcome when faith resides within you. When faced with a challenge, don't embrace the assumption that you will not be the victor over the challenge. Celebrate the lessons learned in the fight against the challenge, while holding strong to the belief that you will be triumphant over the challenge. My friend, any challenge is simply a humbling experience that strengthens your faith in the power of God. The Lord makes the challenges you have today become your testimonies in the times ahead.

For testimonies to be the product of the obstacles in your life, faith must live within you, even when you face your biggest challenges. Don't contaminate your blessings by focusing upon what did not turn out well for you in the past. My friend, the past is just that...the past. Let what has happened previously in your life remain in the past. You can't let your mind live in the negative points of yesterday if you want God to bless you today, and in the days ahead.

> **"It's better to look ahead and prepare than to look back and regret."**
> —Jackie Joyner Kersee

No matter what obstacle stands before you, prepare for your test against that obstacle to become a testimony. If the testimony you need of God's greatness involves your health, keep the faith that God will work the situation out in your favor. Even if the doctor told you that you only have a few months to live, still keep the faith. Proclaim that the hand of God will move in your favor. Affirm that the hand of God will move in your favor. Your medical situation may be incurable because man can't fix it, but *all* is curable through God.

If the testimony you need of God's greatness involves your employment, keep the faith that God will work the situation out in your favor. Proclaim that the hand of God will move in your favor. Affirm that the hand of God will move in your favor. After receiving one second of God's favor, you are able to go from being "just another worker" to a high-ranking executive.

Always keep the faith that whatever test you are going through *will* become a testimony for you. There is nothing that you need that is not within your reach. No matter what may be taking place in your life, look at your situation through the eyes of faith. All it takes is the blink of an eye to be blessed when you have faith. When you close your eyes at night, see faith. When you open your eyes in the morning, see faith. When you listen to the sounds around you, let faith ring out of your ears. In all that you do, keep the faith! The eyes of faith are upon your blessings, all the livelong day! Today is *your* day!

ABOUT THE AUTHOR

Passion. Persistence. Perseverance. These three words shape how Vempre Terrell, Jr. continually strives to positively impact individuals throughout the nation. As a dynamic motivational speaker, Vempre reaches out to audiences who often have a need for encouragement, as well as those who enjoy listening to inspirational words being spoken. By bringing spiritual guidance together with self-empowerment, Vempre has encouraged his listeners to accept a fulfilling view of themselves. In his words, "All it takes is the blink of an eye to be blessed when you have faith."

www.ingramcontent.com/pod-product-compliance
Lightning Source LLC
Chambersburg PA
CBHW070110120526
44588CB00032B/1406